A DAILY LECTIONARY

A DAILY LECTIONARY

Scripture Readings for Every Day Based
on the New Common Lectionary

PSALMS SELECTIONS BY THOMAS R. HAWKINS

W. Douglas Mills

THE UPPER ROOM
Nashville, Tennessee

A Daily Lectionary

Copyright © 1986 by The Upper Room. All rights reserved.

No part of this book may be reproduced in any manner whatsoever without written permission of the publisher except in brief quotations embodied in critical articles or reviews. For information address The Upper Room, 1908 Grand Avenue, P.O. Box 189, Nashville, Tennessee 37202.

Scripture quotations not otherwise identified are from the Revised Standard Version of the Bible, copyrighted 1946, 1952, and © 1971 by the Division of Christian Education, National Council of the Churches of Christ in the United States of America, and are used by permission.

Scripture quotations designated NEB are from *The New English Bible,* © The Delegates of the Oxford University Press and the Syndics of the Cambridge University Press 1961 and 1970, and are used by permission.

Scripture quotations designated KJV are from the King James Version of the Bible.

Common Lectionary: The Lectionary Proposed by the Consultation on Common Texts is published by The Church Hymnal Corporation and © 1983, James M. Schellman.

Book and Cover Design: Nancy Johnstone
First Printing: September 1986 (5)
Library of Congress Catalog Card Number: 86-50918
ISBN: 0-8358-0517-4

Printed in the United States of America

Contents

Preface   7

1. Time and Seasons   11

2. Being Formed by the Word   22

3. Praying the Psalms   36

4. An Invitation   43

5. Year A   51

6. Year B   80

7. Year C   109

Preface

For a period of time, I served as a chapel intern for the divinity school of Duke University. It was my responsibility to choose scripture readings for our daily worship services. As a regular attendant of an Anglican religious order, the Society of St. John the Evangelist, I had the two-year daily lectionary in hand. As a United Methodist minister I had, also, the three-year Sunday lectionary. Unfortunately, the two did not work together, though none can expect that they should. In an effort to remedy this situation, I have compiled this project. The intent of this work is to combine the Sunday lectionary with the daily lectionary design.

The first draft of this project became my masters thesis as I completed a Master of Theology at Duke. The Upper Room was introduced to the idea by my friend Elise Eslinger, whose effervescent excitement was contagious. Elise also introduced me to Thomas Hawkins, without whose knowledge of the Psalms this work would be incomplete.

There are others I wish to thank, though the list is long and I fear I may leave someone off. I am grateful for friends such as Jay, Mark, Red, Laura, and Anna, who helped me type and proofread. I am grateful for Fathers Bob, Tom, and Paul, who were a source of prayer and encouragement. I am especially thankful for three of my professors, Geoffrey Wainwright, Thomas Langford, and Dick Eslinger. They were a constant inspiration to me, though they may not have known it.

A Daily Lectionary

I dedicate this book to Dede Funkhouser. She shared my joys and frustrations. She has been my best friend and greatest source of love. She believed in me, encouraged me, and nearly kept me from finishing.

In Christ's service,

W. Douglas Mills

PART I

1
TIME AND SEASONS

Time directs, shapes, and gives everyone purpose. From spring to summer to fall to winter, people's lives are ordered by the time in which they live. All have time to do that which has significance for them, but less significant things are lost to lack of time. Everyone is identified by what fills time: humans are working, playing, and resting people. Christians are identified by a particular time. Jesus said, "The time is fulfilled, and the kingdom of God is at hand; repent, and believe in the gospel" (Mark 1:15).

Time has purpose, moving from beginning to end. Genesis discloses that time was first marked by God. God divided the darkness from the light, calling the first "night" and the second "day." There was morning and evening, the first day. As the day described by the writer ends, the reader senses an anticipation that the first day was only the beginning. There will be another day, as God has created divisions of time to mark the rising crescendo toward which time moves. So the days pass into weeks, the weeks into months, and the months into years—never pausing and never repeating but always marching forward. Time has beginning with creation, receives direction through the Incarnation, and has end, as always, with God.

In the course of time, God has acted, God's saving presence realized. Christ has entered the world so that all time has become God's time of salvation. God's revelation occurs within the same course of time as the world's events: "The Lord spoke to Moses in the wilderness of Sinai, in the tent of meeting, on the first day of the second month, in the second year after they had come out of the land of Egypt" (Num. 1:1). God is known through time where God has acted in the days, the weeks, and the years of men and women to make self-disclosure. Time is salvation history.

Events flow in only one direction: out of the future, through the present, and into the past. Time has purpose and direction. God gives to time and history a significance in which God's people participate.

Time is not just clock time for God's people. Time has meaning, not as something which is counted and past, but as that which has past, present, and future. Because time is the story of God's action, the meaning of time can only be known in God. God has created a universe that is structured by time, and God relates to that universe in an appropriate temporal mode. As God's people participate in God's time, we find that we are a part of God's story. It is not surprising, then, that Christian worship is structured by time. The Christian church keeps time with God in the way it observes God's weeks, months, and years.

The calendar is the instrument the church uses to divide and measure time and to participate in God's story. Because the Christian calendar is more to the church than a collection of special days, the year itself becomes a way to commemorate and reexperience God's saving acts. The calendar year works like a family photo album by telling the story of who we are. By retelling the story of God in Christ through the liturgical year, the church invites hearers to participate and become a part of the story. The liturgical calendar is not the world's year but the church's year. It is a "Christ-centered whole,"[1] which reminds everyone of the events in the saving work of Christ.

To Remember

At the exit of Yad Vashem, the Holocaust museum in Jerusalem, is a sign in Hebrew that articulates the deep sense of remembrance in Jewish thought. As I remember the sign, an English translation might be, "To forget is exile; remembrance is the secret of redemption." Here, in a sentence, is the essence of remembering, the hope and life of Israel. It is the reason why Israel celebrates the Passover each year. The secret of redemption is recalling—and thereby participating in—the story of God's salvation. To remember is to bring the past into the present in order to hope in the future.

Remembering is not unique to Israel. Every family takes pride in its story, which it remembers and retells on occasion. As at birthdays and anniversaries, remembering and celebrating go hand in hand. Remembering in the context of celebration literally "recalls" the event of the past so that it affects people in the present. Remembering is not retelling simply for the sake of reminiscence. Instead, the past is remembered and recalled because it affects the present. Because time has direction and purpose, "remembering leads us into tomorrow and inserts us into the future."[2]

Israel's celebration of the Passover is the present being affected by the past to give purpose and meaning to the future. The bread of the meal is unleavened because deliverance was in haste, before the dough could rise. It is necessary to chew bitter herbs to recall the hard bondage in Egypt. The fruits and nuts are the remembrance of the mud and work of slavery. The specific character of the meal provides the opportunity to relive the story about how a people became God's people.[3]

In the same way, the meal that Christians eat together is to reexperience before God the first coming of Christ and his sacrifice on Calvary. The Eucharist is celebrated in commemoration of Christ not only because it reminds persons of his saving work, but also because it "recalls before God with thanksgiving that one sacrifice and prays for the continuing benefits of that sacrifice to be granted now."[4]

Worship as a memorial serves to remind humankind of the mercy of God, and it enables the worshiper to recall before God with thanksgiving past deeds and promises. The Eucharist, the Lord's Day, and the liturgical year all tell the story of God at work, thereby claiming God's continuing mercy for the future. Here, the three dimensions of time—past, present, and future—

are joined with purpose. The memorial character of Christian worship gives meaning to and draws the worshipers into the passage of time so that their story becomes a part of God's larger story.

The Calendar in Historical Survey

The Christian calendar begins not with the church year but with the church week. The seven-day week as the basic unit of time in the Christian tradition is a continuation of Jewish custom.[5] In early Christianity, the six days other than the Sabbath, the last day of the week, did not have names but were simply designated numerically.

The heart of the Christian week is the paschal mystery. This mystery embraces the whole of the suffering and death of Christ, from his crucifixion to his burial and eventual resurrection. Though the day had no name, the early church, with little hesitation, adopted the first day of the week as the celebration of the paschal mystery. It was, after all, on the first day of the week that the women found the empty tomb and that the Lord appeared. The day of the Lord's resurrection was the day the early church gathered for worship, to break bread together (Acts 20:7).

The first day of the week is "the heart of the liturgical year" because it is the oldest element of the Christian calendar. It is the original Christian feast; from it the other feasts and seasons evolved.[6] Theologically, the first day encapsulates the whole of the gospel message. The writer of Revelation called it "the Lord's day" (Rev. 1:10), associating it with Christ the Lord. It was not only the day of the Lord's resurrection but, perhaps more importantly, the day on which the early community observed the Lord's Supper.

The weekly celebration of creation and redemption, centered on the paschal mystery and the Lord's Supper, is also the foundation for the entire annual cycle. One Sunday of the year took on special significance as the day for the annual celebration of Christ's death and resurrection. Paul assigned new meaning to the annual Jewish Passover (1 Cor. 5:7-8), writing that Christ has become our paschal lamb and, therefore, the feast should be kept in memory of the Christian mystery. One can assume that the early Jewish-Christian communities "Christianized" the Jewish Passover and remembered it as *the* feast of Christian redemption.

Although the year of the first Easter celebration will never be determined, the appropriate time of its celebration caused the first churchwide controversy. This question of great importance to the church in the second century was whether the annual celebration of redemption should be held on the fourteenth day of Nisan, the first full moon of spring, no matter which day of the week this might be, or whether it should be held on the first Sunday after Nisan 14. The "Quartodecimans" of Asia Minor were so named because they defended the first view. Rome and most of the other local churches, however, stood by the second view. This argument was not settled until the First Ecumenical Council of Nicea in A.D. 325, where it was decided that Easter would be celebrated on the first Sunday after the first full moon of spring. Because Easter is determined by the phase of the moon, it and the first day of the Jewish Passover would never again be celebrated on the same day. The lunar reckoning of Easter also meant that the date of the feast could vary over a five-week period.

The Quartodeciman controversy illuminates two important points. First, while the feast of Easter is not expressly mentioned until the second century, it was being celebrated before then. Second, the documents that have survived detail the liturgy that was part of the feast, which included a eucharistic meal at the end of a period of fasting. Easter was the most important feast of the Christian year for a good reason. Easter is the church's proclamation of the redemptive action of Christ, the conquest of sin and reconciliation of the human race with God.

In the fourth century church, a worship that was more historically oriented was emphasized. A European nun, Egeria, traveled the holy land around A.D. 384, making extensive notes of worship in the churches.[7] The worship of this period attempted to recover the historical events of Jesus' life, especially those of his passion. Thus, on Palm Sunday, all the Christians of Jerusalem were led by the bishop from the Mount of Olives into Jerusalem. Part of this walk included carrying palm or olive branches. Other days in that week also had special significance. On Wednesday, the bishop read about Judas's plot to betray Jesus, and the people groaned and lamented in response. On Thursday, the people led the bishop to Gethsemane; and on Friday, services were held on Golgotha.

Two other seasons became associated with Easter during the fourth century. First, the Quartodeciman controversy gives evidence of a period of fasting before Easter. The First Ecumenical Council of Nicea spoke of a forty-day Lenten period of fasting—symbolic of Jesus' fast in the desert and the number of years Israel wandered in the desert—as if it were common to all. Second, the church, from the second century on, continued the feast of joy and celebration for fifty days after Easter. By the end of the fourth century, Jesus' ascension was accepted as the fortieth day after Easter (Acts 1:3) and the descent of the Spirit, ten days later (Acts 2), that is, on the fiftieth day, or Pentecost.[8]

The time periods from Lent through Easter and from Easter to Pentecost were theologically and historically tied together. By the fourth century these cycles were inseparable, each event depending on the other for its fullest meaning. The events of this cycle derived from the Easter festival and, as a whole, proclaimed the saving work of God in Christ. Through its worship in this way, the church reparticipated in God's story. This Christ-centered cycle of Easter commemorated the saving action of Christ on the cross. It is not surprising that the church should celebrate also his birth and incarnation.

The origin of the Christmas cycle is obscure. While December 25 was recognized by Rome as the birth date of Jesus by A.D. 336, the Eastern church had long since considered January 6 as the Epiphany of the Lord. For the West, December 25 commemorated Jesus' birth; in the East, Jesus' birth and baptism were celebrated on January 6. In the historicizing movement of the fourth century, East and West "borrowed" each other's feast,[9] and the outcome was the celebration of Jesus' birth on December 25 and his baptism and the coming of the Magi on January 6.

Since January 6 was an important day for baptism in the Eastern church, a period of preparation like Lent was common. Sources describing the length of Advent or the time when it was first introduced are rare. The first traces of an observance of Advent come from the area of Spain, influenced by the Eastern church, where Advent was a three-week period of fasting. Some areas, including Gaul, observed a six-week Advent. The Roman church eventually reduced the season to four weeks, though this position was not accepted completely until the tenth or eleventh centuries.

Overall, the church's calendar had its shape by the end of the fourth century. The Christian year is not like a pie cut into equal portions with many days of equal importance continuing in a never-ending cycle. Christian time moves forward with purpose rather than in a circle of repetition. The Christian year has two Christological cycles: Advent-Christmas-Epiphany and Lent-Easter-Pentecost. Some days are "high" days bursting with joy; other days are somber. The Christian year is the church's way of retelling God's story. St. John Chrysostom of the fourth century summarized the church year in terms of paschal mystery:

> Had Christ not been born in the flesh, he would not have been baptized, which is the Theophany or Manifestation; nor would he have been crucified, which is the Pasch; nor would he have sent down the Spirit, which is Pentecost.[10]

The church retells the Gospel story, inviting hearers to participate.

The Contemporary Calendar

The history of the church calendar since its formulation around the fourth century has been one of continual addition and subtraction. For the most part, these additions have been saint's days and feasts of Mary. Some idea feasts were added also, including a feast of the Holy Trinity and, in 1925, the feast of Christ the King. Many feasts were questioned by Protestant reformers, and even in the Roman church they have been subjected to a series of reforms. What has been left for modern times is the basic structure developed in the early church.

The history and tradition of the calendar is interesting. Essentially, the calendar is the way in which the church in any era chooses to present the gospel story within the bounds of time. Each subsequently revised calendar has met with both criticisms and affirmations. While neither the calendar of the earliest church nor that of the medieval church is more authoritative, the modern church does want to claim that part of Christian tradition that facilitates the hearing of God's saving work in its most meaningful form. The church recovers those aspects of its tradition that let shine new light on God's message and that most help it to participate in God's time.

For the first time since the Reformation, the modern church has a genuinely ecumenical calendar which is accepted by a majority of Christians throughout the world. This situation is largely due to the reforms and new directions arising within the Roman Catholic church after Vatican II. The new calendar that resulted from Vatican II went into effect in 1970. Most of its reforms have been adopted by Protestant denominations because it makes the best use of time for telling the biblical story. Recovering the tradition of the early church, this new calendar emphasizes God's actions in history and the continuing work of the Holy Spirit. It is void of time for recognition of human agency and achievement and thus makes sound theological sense, even to Protestants.

This new calendar (and resultant lectionary) is not without its critics. Change is sometimes slow in coming. The strongest complaint has come about from the "elimination" of half the seasons: Epiphany, Pentecost, and Kingdomtide.[11] Most of the confusion surrounding this results from a misunderstanding of the meaning of the seasons. Pentecost is fifty days by definition, so it seems absurd to extend it for half a year. Yet it makes sense to have a season *after* Pentecost. Kingdomtide is the result of a social gospel theology that stresses human activity and is thus eliminated for theological reasons. Epiphany is *a* manifestation, but, again, it makes sense to have a season *after* the Epiphany. In its final form, the new calendar is grounded in the two Christological cycles.[12]

The liturgical year begins with the first Sunday of Advent. This season focuses our attention on the past and future comings of Christ. It prepares us for the Christmas message of God's Incarnation coming into human history. Advent ends with Christmas, which Christian and non-Christian alike observe in one way or another. The paschal mystery finds expression in Christmas, with the focus on the marvelous exchange in the Incarnation of Jesus Christ who gave himself for us (Titus 2:14).

It is unfortunate that, after all the preparation for Christmas, we allow the mood to die the next day. The Christian calendar, on the other hand, continues Christmas through the liturgical week of feasts (an octave) and concludes the next Sunday with the oldest of Christian festivals, Epiphany. The season after Epiphany stresses the various ways in which the Christ has made God manifest to humans. Beginning with Jesus' baptism, the season ends with the Transfiguration.

Lent is a season that derived from the baptismal practices of Easter. Historically, Lent has had several forms and lengths, but it has finally settled into the forty days (excluding Sundays) before Easter. It is a time of preparation, of self-scrutiny, and for consideration of the self-giving nature of the love of Christ, culminating with Christ's passion and death. The Easter season begins Easter Eve as the church anticipates anew the celebration of the Resurrection. The Easter season lasts through the Great Fifty Days until the Day of Pentecost.

The season after Pentecost is the long interim of the new covenant church and is regarded as Ordinary Time. The Sundays of Ordinary Time acquire their liturgical and theological complexion primarily from the readings assigned them in the new lectionary. The Christian year comes to a triumphant close on the Sunday of Christ the King. The very next Sunday begins a new year with the first Sunday in Advent, and the church recalls its past in its application to the present to offer hope for the future.

Notes

1. *Word and Table*, Supplemental Worship Resource 3 (Nashville: Abingdon, 1980), 46.
2. Tad Guzie, "Liturgical Year: What Does it Mean to Remember," *The Church Gives Thanks and Remembers*, ed. Lawrence J. Johnson (Collegeville, MN: The Liturgical Press, 1984), 37ff.
3. Max Thurian, *The Eucharistic Memorial: Part 1-The Old Testament*, Ecumenical Studies in Worship, No. 7 (Richmond, VA: John Knox Press, 1960), 19.
4. Geoffrey Wainwright, *Eucharist and Eschatology* (London: Epworth Press, 1978), 67.
5. Adolf Adam, *The Liturgical Year*, trans. Matthew J. O'Connell (New York: Pueblo, 1981), 7ff.
6. Mark Searle, "Sunday: The Heart of the Liturgical Year," *The Church Gives Thanks and Remembers*, 13.
7. *Egeria's Travels to the Holy Land*, trans. John Wilkinson, rev. ed. (Jerusalem: Ariel Publishing House, 1981).
8. *Seasons of the Gospel*, Supplementary Worship Resource 6 (Nashville: Abingdon, 1979), 19ff.; also Adam, *The Liturgical Year*, 84ff.
9. cf., A. Allan McArthur, *The Evolution of the Christian Year* (London: SCM, 1953), 31f. for the problems with this argument.
10. St. John Chrysostom, "Homily VI," *On the Incomprehensible Nature of God*, trans. Paul W. Harkins (Washington: The Catholic University of America Press, 1984), 175.
11. Edwin B. Womack, "Two Chapters or the Whole Story?" *Circuit Rider*, January 1984, 5.
12. James White, "New Seasons for Worship," *Circuit Rider*, February 1983, 4.

2
BEING FORMED BY THE WORD

"All who desire the grace of God are to wait for it in searching the Scriptures," said John Wesley in his sermon "The Means of Grace."[1] By an individual's reading, hearing, and meditating on the scripture, God has an open channel through which to speak to and by which to convey grace upon him or her. God's story, contained in scripture, is the story that creates the community of God's people. Scripture articulates the fundamental relationship of people with God and with one another. Hearing the word again, as it has been heard in all times past, the people of God are formed in God's call of election, God's judgment of transgression, and God's word of reconciliation.

The people of God share in common the family heritage of the past that is recalled at celebrations and anniversaries. This is the story that has brought believers into the present and that leads them into tomorrow. The story told in scripture is the story of the family of Christians as it struggled to come into being, as it rejoiced in its conquests, as it cried in its sorrows, and as it found hope in being God's people. It is in the story of scripture that Christians discover who they are and who they are meant to be.

The language of scripture is the language of prayer. Believers recall the mighty acts of God that scripture reveals as the secret of human redemption. God acted to redeem the family of believers from Egypt, again to redeem the family in Babylon, and again when God's son lay in a grave. God's mercy endures forever; on this the members of God's family trust that God will redeem them.

The clearest example of scripture as the language of prayer is in the Psalms. The Psalter is a record of the family at prayer. In these prayers, the family members hear voices of praise, thanksgiving, complaint, anguish, trust, and awe, which sound not only like the voices of the family but also like the voice of each individual.

Daily Prayer

Daily prayer was the rule of practice in the Jewish synagogues and, consequently, was probably the practice in the early Christian community. Luke summarizes the life of the early church in Jerusalem as one in which its members persevered in the teaching and fellowship of the apostles, in the breaking of bread, and in the prayers (Acts 2:42). Because the earliest Christian community understood that part of its task was prayer, by the end of the first century all believers were instructed to say the Lord's Prayer three times a day (Didache 8:3).

The New Testament writers believed there are specific times of the day that are appropriate for prayer. Luke reports that Peter and John went to the temple at the hour of prayer, three o'clock in the afternoon (Acts 3:1). Even the Gentile, Cornelius, kept this time of prayer (Acts 10:3). Peter had his vision of the clean and unclean animals during the noon hour of prayer (Acts 10:9).

The first Christians had an accepted rhythm, inherited from their Jewish ancestry, to their times of prayer. This rhythm included not only the ninth hour (3:00 P.M.), the sixth hour (noon), and the third hour (9:00 A.M.), but also early morning and late evening to correspond to the times of the morning and evening sacrifice.

In the tradition of the church, daily prayer has become synonymous with the daily office. Contemporary Christians have been introduced to it through the communities of monks who have the daily office as their set pattern of prayer. Nevertheless, the daily office also presents a certain tension within the church's tradition. The history of the daily office is a long and detailed problem which scholars have not settled completely. It includes the public gatherings of communities of Christians for daily prayer as well as individuals or communities establishing fixed hours for private prayer. We may call the public gatherings of the early church for daily prayer the cathedral office and the private gatherings of the monks the monastic office.

Apart from the Sunday service of Eucharist (Holy Communion), the church originally gathered for public worship twice a day, in the evening and in the morning. Frequently, another service was scheduled on the eves of Sundays and major festivals, but the basic pattern of two public gatherings remained the model until monastic influences changed it.

The monastic movement was a development that sprang from the laity in the church who set themselves apart from the world in order to practice with all intensity the call of unceasing prayer. The dedication to constant prayer required more than two services a day, so the early monks lived a devotional life that was based on other precedents for daily prayer. There are numerous warrants and precedents for any number of scheduled times for prayer, including two, three, five, seven, or eight daily times for prayer. However, these monastic rounds were established for the edification of the individual more than for the community to join in unison adoration.

The shape of the monastic office was constructed primarily for meditation, while the cathedral office was constructed more for public supplication and adoration of the present Christ. In fact, the public office was shaped much like the eucharistic liturgy, without the service at the table. Daily prayer as we know it is a fusion of the public cathedral office and the more private monastic office.

The importance of listening to the word of God has been recognized in Protestant circles as well. John Wesley commended his followers to practice this at least twice a day.[2] Wesley knew that such has always been the practice of the church in its desire to pray without ceasing. In the practice of praying the daily offices, scripture has always been at the center. Listening to the word of God facilitates a deeper level of response to the Lord. To this end, a daily lectionary is required to provide an orderly sequence of lessons that, in time, cover the whole of God's story and call the believers into it to make God's story their story.

The Historical Development of Lectionaries

At Vatican II the Roman Catholic church asked for a new Sunday lectionary. A new calendar was the preliminary step in the process. The Second Vatican Council decided that, in worship, "the treasures of the Bible should be opened more lavishly so that richer fare might be provided for the faithful at the table of God's Word. In this way a more representative portion of sacred Scripture will be read to the people over a set cycle of years."[3] The strength of the new church calendar is its grasp of the central portion of Christian experience and its ability to reflect the vivid message of biblical salvation. The strength of a lectionary based on such a church year is its recovery of scripture as central to Christian faith. This principle that affirms the importance of scripture is attractive also to Protestants, and the resultant ecumenical lectionary is a symbol of Christ's prayer that "all may be one" (John 17:21, KJV).

A lectionary based on the Christian cycle of festivals reflects the very nature of our relationship with God as presented in scripture. When the acts of God are reiterated year after year and day after day, praise of God is deepened. Believers are saved from a false spirituality based on works rather than on God's mighty acts. A lectionary is needed for all the people of God to recover a sense of community and, mostly, to recover a sense of continuity in the sweep of time. Daily time is sanctified by the reliving of God's claim upon history. Even private worship in common with the whole church, made possible by a church year and ecumenical lectionary, keeps prayer from being individualistic. Such a lectionary is an aid to spiritual formation, a way to "proclaim the death of the Lord, until he comes" (1 Cor. 11:26, NEB), and a way to recover valid worship of God.

An orderly sequence of scripture selections used in the public worship of a religious community is not new. The synagogue is the most likely origin of weekly readings.[4] Some scholars even argue that New Testament books, such as Mark or Matthew, are simply a collection of pericopes once assigned in some form to a liturgical year. The synagogue model of cyclical readings developed in ancient and medieval times into lectionaries among Christian communities. The Apostolic Constitutions of the fourth century clearly refers to a five-lesson sequence.

The Council of Trent fixed the Roman lectionary in 1570 by using those readings that had evolved with meaning over a thousand years. The Anglican lectionary, based on the Roman readings, also went through a period of change. Archbishop Cranmer revised the Roman Breviary into the Book of Common Prayer.[5] Three scripture lessons were assigned for morning prayer and two lessons for evening. However, the lectionary was detached from the church year and began on January 1. The orderly reading of scripture was the chief function of the daily offices in the 1549 *Book of Common Prayer*.

John Wesley, who used the Anglican *Book of Common Prayer*, was certainly aware of the benefits of a lectionary. In 1784 when Wesley responded to the desperate cry for help in the new American states, he sent his revisions of the Anglican rites. Wesley's *Sunday Service* was intended to be the Book of Worship for the recently born Methodists. In this extensive service, Wesley provided proper lessons to be read at morning and evening prayer on the Sundays through the year. Wesley assumed that more than one lesson would be read, though how many lessons more is not indicated. His lectionary provided only that the first lesson be used at both services, except Easter Sunday, Whitsunday, Trinity Sunday, Christmas, Good Friday, and Ascension Day, for which he provided two lessons apiece. That Wesley provided a New Testament reading as the second lesson for these days is evidence that Wesley expected more than one lesson, but probably only two, to be used regularly in worship.

The Ecumenical Sunday Lectionary

The decision by the Roman Catholic church at Vatican II to open more lavishly the rich fare of God's word led to some of the most radical changes in the long, long history of the lectionary. More than simply updating, the Council fathers set out many reforms. The eighteen members of this group assigned to work on the lectionary were instructed to make proposals, which they did only after years of biblical studies, experimentation, and revisions. The fathers studied existing pericope systems and sought the advice of many biblical scholars. A rough draft was complete by 1967 and revisions made in 1968. The final product was decreed to begin on November 30, 1969. The new order of readings was based on a three-year cycle in which three readings—an Old Testament, a Gospel and an epistle—were assigned.

Since many Protestants had been consulted in the development of this new lectionary, the lectionary immediately caught the interest of Protestant denominations. Hailed by some as the finest lectionary in Christian history, it was natural that other traditions adopt much of it. The Episcopal church first used a revision of it in the *Book of Common Prayer* of 1970. The Presbyterian Church in the United States and the United Presbyterian Church in the United States of America also adopted it, with revisions, in 1970. Other denominations followed suit.

In the fall of 1972, the Consultation on Church Union (COCU) Commission on Worship began work on a lectionary to serve as a symbol of church unity and as an aid to those churches without a recent lectionary.[6] The first necessity before the commission, the adoption of a calendar, resulted in the acceptance of the calendar outlined above. The commission then aligned the four common lectionaries (Roman Catholic, Episcopal, Presbyterian, and Lutheran) in parallel columns according to Sunday and season. The lectionary that was put forth by the commission is a consensus using the lections on which sources agreed or, if the sources did not agree, using the lection that best fit the sequence. Duplications were avoided. The product follows the Roman calendar, a three-year cycle, and three readings per Sunday system.

Final approval was given to the COCU lectionary in 1974. Meanwhile, the Section on Worship of the United Methodist Board of Discipleship had begun work on new worship resources. Seeing no reason to recommend a lectionary other than the COCU one, the section proposed its use among United Methodists. Responding to the desire that a Psalter be included, Hoyt Hickman and James White prepared a consensus Psalter for the COCU committee, which was adopted and included in the package for United Methodists.

Part of the struggle to be a more vital and faithful church is the ongoing reform and renewal of worship. Renewal is a good sign of a healthy and lively faith. It signals, at every turn, the discovery of Christ in the life of the church and in the mission of the church in the world. Though the time has been short since the introduction of the lectionary, United Methodists now are given the opportunity to accept a refinement of that lectionary. The previous lectionary was very good; none of the older lectionaries, especially those on a cycle of one or two years, could match the new order in terms of approach, coverage, and balanced treatment of biblical material. Indeed, the success of the new calendar and lectionary was greater than had ever been anticipated. However, the developers of the COCU lectionary had intended all along to reconsider their work after two full cycles. Critiques of the methodology and the ecumenical state allowed evaluation to happen sooner.

In 1978 the Consultation on Common Texts (CCT) created a committee to revise the lectionary. "The guidelines were clear: create a consensus calendar and lectionary for all three years, do not disturb the Gospel lesson arrangement except in very special circumstances, and retain the principle of thematic correlation on festival days and during the Advent/Epiphany and Lent/Easter cycles."[7] The ecumenical committee produced a polished consensus lectionary for Sunday worship services, which was introduced to The United Methodist Church on the first Sunday of Advent, 1983.[8]

Lectionary Criticisms

Lectionaries as a whole have met with considerable criticism.[9] The most verbal complaint comes from preachers and worship leaders who feel that freedom in worship has been sacrificed. The pastor is the hinge on which the community revolves around the scripture. Ideally it is the pastor's job to relate the context of the community to the identity of the faithful as it is shaped by the canon; therefore, imposed lections may be at odds with congregational needs. However, lack of biblical knowledge, theological misperception, pastoral subjectivity, and a host of other issues keep this ideal from being reality. A minister who reads and preaches from a well-balanced lectionary covers most major biblical themes and is forced away from redundant, but favorite, themes. Lectionary preaching is good discipline.

Another criticism of a three-reading lectionary is the often strained relationship between texts. In the Christological cycles, the Gospel lesson ideally determines a theme to which the Old Testament lesson and sometimes the epistle lesson relate. In reality, the relation is sometimes awkward. Also, there are many Old Testament themes that cannot be matched with a New Testament text. This problem is alleviated if a greater portion of the Old Testament is used and if all realize that it is not necessary for all the lessons to be in congruence.

There will always be doubt among some that the integrity of the whole of scripture can be preserved with a lectionary that, of necessity, must exclude portions of scripture. This is a particularly crucial question in regard to the Old Testament. Choosing only themes that are congruent with New Testament texts, and then only by allusion or incidental matter, does not allow important thrusts of the Old Testament to be discovered. Congruence itself deprives the canon of its strength in diversity. In response, it must be said over and over that, while lectionaries are a positive and extremely useful tool, they cannot substitute completely for a study of the Bible in toto. There is a sense in which a lectionary will be of greatest value only when it is projected against the whole of scripture.

Methodology for a Daily Lectionary

In the historical review of the ecumenical calendar and lectionary and the theological justification for the use of both of these, certain methodologies have surfaced, which govern the development of a lectionary. It must be kept in mind that the lectionary (COCU or CCT) in use in United Methodism and ecumenical circles is a lectionary primarily of Sunday, eucharistic texts. What is not to be found in the ecumenical arena or in United Methodism in particular is a lectionary of daily biblical lessons.

If the number of Bible study guides, lay helps for biblical interpretation, and small group studies is any indication, then there is certainly a revival of interest in studying the word of God at its source. Several quarters have heard the call for biblical preaching and others have heeded the desire for scripture-centered Sunday school literature. The body of believers wants to reclaim its scriptural identity and discover its biblical roots. Men and women everywhere are asking for a guide to Bible reading, and all the reasons cited for the acceptability of liturgical renewal are motivation enough to provide for this need. A program of Bible study would indeed further discipline, foster spiritual formation, emphasize God's gift of salvation while reevaluating human achievement, and give substance to the unity of the church.

The methodology used in past calendar and lectionary developments can, with additions and revisions, be used to attain this goal of an ecumenical daily lectionary.

1. It is important and necessary to follow the Christian church calendar. This insures the reading of the full sequence of God's mighty acts. Our present calendar, pivoting on two Christological cycles, is the most refined system enabling us to "know nothing . . . except Jesus Christ and him crucified" (1 Cor. 2:2). Our calendar presents the whole story of God's self-disclosure, from God's calling of Israel to God's calling of the New Testament church in Christ.

Two corallaries go along with this first principle:

a. Civic and national holidays are to be omitted from the course of readings. Not only do these holidays detract from the ecumenicity and catholicity of a lectionary, but civic festivals tend to emphasize the good works of humankind as opposed to the gracious acts of God. Even within Methodism, the entire denomination is not geographically limited to one country, so some civic holidays have no meaning in other parts of the church. Furthermore, the church within one country needs to reexamine its observance of some holidays. While we may not be able to stop the recognition of American Independence Day, we do not need to turn that into idolatrous worship of civil religion.

    b. It is necessary to reach an agreement on dating in the Christian calendar. For the most part, all are in agreement that the church year begins with Advent. The CCT lectionary committee has reached general agreement with other trouble areas, also. Lutherans had adopted a different method of dating Sundays after Pentecost causing some summer lessons to be "off," or different from the Roman Catholic, Episcopalian, and United Methodist systems by two or three weeks. Agreement must be had that requires the renumbering of Ordinary Time before the season of Lent to account for the movable date of Easter.

    2. Traditions which already have a daily lectionary are also using the ecumenical Sunday lectionary, thus presenting two sets of texts assigned on Sundays. The Sunday texts from the individual daily lectionaries do not coincide with the Sunday eucharistic texts from the CCT or COCU lectionaries. To alleviate this problem, the Sunday eucharistic lections need to be the definitive assignment. This may create problems in traditions that have morning and evening prayer as well as a eucharistic service. That concern needs study and experimentation; innovations may be the answer. In the meantime, the eucharistic texts should stand as the Sunday assignment.

    3. It is traditional that certain books be associated with certain seasons. Lessons chosen for Lent reflect the ancient practice of preparation for baptism, for example. Job and Jonah have long been associated with Good Friday. The COCU lectionary has even convinced us that in the three-year cycle, Matthew

is associated with year A, Mark with year B, Luke with year C, and John interspersed in the Christological cycles. The CCT lectionary goes even further to associate the Pentateuch and Mosaic narratives with year A, the Davidic narrative with year B, and the Elijah-Elisha narratives along with wisdom literature with year C. There are good reasons for these associations but none are above review. Nevertheless, some recognition of this must be maintained in a daily lectionary.

4. Although lectionaries of different churches have not always been the same, two related principles govern the selection of texts:

    a. The best lectionary in terms of coverage is a *lectio continua*. Continuous reading of a biblical book facilitates complete encounter. As a general rule, continuous readings are to be the norm for a daily lectionary.

    b. A *lectio continua* makes the best sense during Ordinary Time of the calendar. During the Christological cycles (Advent-Epiphany, Lent-Easter), thematic correlation between Gospel and Old Testament lections allows users to see the interrelatedness of scripture. Granted, the congruity of themes must be considered carefully. Still, relatedness is important. In a daily lectionary, not all three lessons must be congruent, though that is preferable. Furthermore, when the Sunday theme will be continued for several days, the divergent and converse themes would make for a well-balanced treatment.

5. The three-year cycle and a three-reading assignment are not historical requirements. Both criteria make logistical sense, however. A daily lectionary on a two-year cycle cannot be governed by the three-year Sunday readings of the ecumenical lectionary.

6. Existing daily lectionaries need to be consulted. Just as the COCU and CCT lectionaries are consensus lectionaries, so must a daily lectionary attempt to incorporate the best of several traditions. Daily lectionary development will be encumbered by the fact that there is little agreement between existing lection-

aries, especially since most are on a two-year cycle. Consensus can be a guide, though impossible at times.

7. Pericopes must be defined by careful scholarship. "Scholarship" leaves much room for criticism and doubt; yet, there are guiding principles to be observed. Textual devices used by the biblical writers to note pericope beginnings and endings should be given control. Choppy readings which omit verses midsequence should be expanded to include those verses. Lections need not be unreasonably long; neither should lections be tailored to meet preconceived notions of thought nor cut in such a way that a unit is interrupted.

8. The last item will be subject to the most criticism. It has four parts:

   a. During seasons of thematic association between lessons, the Gospel lesson is to be the controlling text. This idea is not contrary to the method used for the ecumenical lectionaries now available.

   b. In those seasons of thematic association, the controlling Sunday lections need to govern thematically over a period of several days. The Sunday theme could be continued through the following Saturday with the next Sunday beginning a new theme. Perhaps a better idea is to use Wednesday as a "swing" day so that a theme is continued from Wednesday through Tuesday with the controlling Sunday lections coming in the middle. This would provide a period of anticipation of the Sunday lections, followed by a time of review. Creativity might be useful in this system to include texts that are related by virtue of opposite or divergent themes. Such a method using this anticipation/continuance idea provides a better balanced lectionary.

   c. Certain weeks constitute an octave and these days should guide the selection of texts. Holy Week is such an octave and traditional texts are associated with each day of that week. Other such octaves occur after Christmas and after Easter.

   d. Repetition is to be minimized. This will be best accomplished by observing a *lectio continua* when the season allows for it.

A daily lectionary based upon such methodology would be compatible with the CCT lectionary and would be easily accessible for those using the Sunday eucharistic readings.

Notes

1. John Wesley, "The Means of Grace," *Works* (Grand Rapids, MI: Baker Book House, 1978 [rep. of 1872]), 5: 192.

2. John Wesley, "Explanatory Notes on the Old Testament," *Works*, 14: 252-53.

3. Constitution on Sacred Liturgy, Article 51.

4. John Reumann, "A History of Lectionaries: From the Synagogue at Nazareth to Post–Vatican II," *Interpretation* 31 (April 1977): 118.

5. G. J. Cuming, "The Office in the Church of England," *The Study of Liturgy*, ed. Cheslyn Jones, et al. (New York: Oxford, 1978), 390.

6. Consultation on Church Union, Commission on Worship, *A Lectionary* (Princeton, 1974), 2.

7. Richard L. Eslinger, "Introducing the New Common Lectionary," *Worship Alive!*, Discipleship Resources W115L, 2.

8. James M. Schellman, *Common Lectionary: The Lectionary Proposed by the Consultation on Common Texts* (New York: Church Hymnal Corporation, 1983).

9. cf. Lloyd R. Bailey, "The Lectionary in Critical Perspective," *Interpretation* 31 (April 1977): 139-153.

3
PRAYING THE PSALMS

By Thomas R. Hawkins

"Lord, teach us to pray," asked the disciples. So Jesus instructed the tiny band of followers how to pray. We also need someone to teach us to pray. In countless yearnings and questionings we ask, "Lord, teach us to pray." The psalms are one of the ways in which our Lord teaches us to pray. The church has always perceived this, sometimes clearly and sometimes dimly, and has treated the psalms differently from other scripture. Lessons from the Hebrew Bible, the epistles, and the Gospels are read to a listening congregation. The people themselves, however, have sung or read together the psalms. That is, they have prayed the psalm rather than listened to it as a scripture lesson.

When first learning a foreign language, classes learn by repetition. French instructors point to an apple and say, "*pomme.*" The class repeats after him or her, "*pomme.*" Eventually students graduate to sentences. "*Fahren wir nach Köln,*" the German professor says. And the class automatically responds, "*Fahren wir nach Köln.*" So also is it with prayer. We learn to pray by repeating those prayers that God has prayed on the creation's behalf. "So we learn to speak to God because God has spoken to us and speaks to us. . . . Repeating God's own words after him, we begin to pray to him," writes Dietrich Bonhoeffer in his little book *Psalms: The Prayer Book of the Bible.*[1]

Prayer, Bonhoeffer goes on to say, is neither to stand speechless before God nor simply to pour out our heart before God. It is "to find the way to God and to speak with him, whether the heart is full or empty."[2] Sometimes our lives are so conflicted and blocked that we cannot formulate our own prayers. We can neither identify our feelings, thoughts, and emotions nor give them a coherent shape and meaning. At other times we have too many things to say to God. We confuse the jumble of our hopes, wishes, laments, and rejoicings—all of which our hearts can do by themselves, as Bonhoeffer so perceptively notes—with prayer. By praying the psalms we learn how to pray when we feel that we have nothing to say to God. By praying the psalms we discover how to cut through the many diversions and false paths and to grasp what is essential in our prayer.

The psalms can do this for us because, rather than speaking to us, they speak for us. The fourth-century pastor and theologian Athanasius once wrote to his friend Marcellinus, explaining why the psalms are so important as we learn to pray. In the other scripture, Athanasius proposes, we hear what we must do or what others have done. We listen to what the prophets said about the Messiah. We listen to what the apostles told about Jesus. The Psalter, however, "contains even the emotions of each soul, and it has the changes and rectifications of these delineated and regulated in itself." When the Christian recites the psalms, he or she "comprehends and is taught in it the emotions of the soul, and, consequently, on the basis of that which affects him and by which he is constrained, he also is enabled by this book to possess the image deriving from the words."[3]

In other scripture, we marvel at the deeds of the prophets or of Jesus; but readers always "consider themselves to be other than those about whom the passage speaks, so that they only come to the imitation of the deeds that are told to the extent that they marvel at them and desire to emulate them." When the Christian recites the psalms, however, he or she recognizes these words "as being his own words. And the one who hears is deeply moved, as though he himself were speaking, and is affected by the words of the songs, as if they were his own songs."[4] The psalms introduce us to our conformity to Christ rather than presenting him for our imitation.

A Daily Lectionary

When we pray the psalms, we are reminded that we are never alone with God. Our psalm-prayers are always offered with and for other Christians and on behalf of the whole cosmos. They are first the prayers of the whole community; they are only secondly our private prayers. The psalms are first the prayers of the community of Israel; only secondly are they our private prayers. Even if our rhythm of daily prayer is a personal one, the praying of the psalms reminds us that our prayer is corporate and joins us to the whole people of God.

The Psalms component of the following lectionary is designed with these theological and devotional perspectives in mind. The psalms have been arranged so that they can be prayed meaningfully in the context of the other daily readings. The themes, which emerge naturally from the scripture readings, flow into the prayers that we seek to offer to God. The psalms have been selected so that they can be prayed in the light of these reflections and meditations. Since repetition and familiarity help shape our spirits and hearts, each psalm is repeated at least four times each year, once from Advent to Epiphany, once from Lent to Pentecost, and twice in Ordinary Time. Because of the fixed number of psalms and the varying number of days in each quarter, some psalms will recur more than once each quarter.

In some cases the connections between the psalms and the other readings will be self-evident. Psalms 22 and 69, for example, are used with the passion narratives. Psalm 2 ("You are my son, today I have begotten you") is linked to the birth narratives or to themes of resurrection and of ascension. In year B/proper 26, the Hebrew lesson concerns Jeremiah's confrontation with the royal court and his imprisonment. Psalm 142, sometimes called the "prisoner's psalm," gathers up these emotions and thoughts:

> In the path where I walk
>   they have hidden a trap for me.
> I look to the right and watch,
>   but there is none who takes notice of me;

> no refuge remains to me,
> no man cares for me.
>
> I cry to thee, O Lord;
> I say, Thou art my refuge,
> my portion in the land of the living.
> Give heed to my cry;
> for I am brought very low!
>
> Deliver me from my persecutors;
> for they are too strong for me!
> Bring me out of prison,
> that I may give thanks to thy name!
> The righteous will surround me;
> for thou wilt deal bountifully with me.
> —142:3b-7

In year C/proper 8, Luke 9:51-62 recalls how the disciples want to call down fire on a village that refuses hospitality. Psalm 58 contains imprecations and violent passions that remind us of the inner demons of resentment and vengeance with which the disciples contended and with which we also must contend:

> O God, break the teeth in their mouths;
> tear out the fangs of the young lions, O Lord!
> Let them vanish like water that runs away
> like grass let them be trodden down and wither.
> Let them be like the snail which dissolves into slime,
> like the untimely birth that never sees the sun.
> Sooner than your pots can feel the heat of thorns,
> whether green or ablaze, may he sweep them away!
> —58:6-9

When the Hebrew lesson deals with Nehemiah's inspection of Jerusalem, the Psalms of Zion (Psalms 46, 48, 84, 87) help us pray and experience something of what Nehemiah felt and prayed.

At other times the connections are less apparent. Psalm 81,

for instance, derives from the context of Israel's covenant renewal festival. It is, therefore, appropriate to link it to Solomon's speech in 1 Kings 8 that deals with covenant renewal themes. In year C/proper 12, the Wednesday readings speak of Mary and also of King Manasseh. Thus the morning and evening psalms contrast these two figures. Psalm 36 reflects upon evil and sin and relates to the Deuteronomic historian's perspective on the "sin of Manasseh":

> Transgression speaks to the wicked
>   deep in his heart;
>   there is no fear of God
>   before his eyes.
>
> For he flatters himself in his own eyes
>   that his iniquity cannot be found out and hated.
> The words of his mouth are mischief and deceit;
>   he has ceased to act wisely and do good.
> He plots mischief while on his bed;
>   he sets himself in a way that is not good;
>   he spurns not evil.
>   —36:1-4

Psalm 123 gathers into itself the inner sense of Mary's self-understanding:

> Behold, as the eyes of servants
>   look to the hand of their master,
> as the eyes of a maid
>   to the hand of her mistress,
> so our eyes look to the Lord our God,
>   till he have mercy upon us.
>   —123:2

Elsewhere, Psalm 29 ("The voice of the Lord is upon the waters. . . . The Lord sits enthroned over the flood") is linked to the narratives of how Jesus stilled the storm.

This approach to psalm selection has, for the most part,

Praying the Psalms

preserved the traditional categories of morning and evening psalms. Each day suggests two psalms: one for morning use, the second for evening. In most cases the historical psalms of the daily office have retained their morning or evening identification. Occasionally, however, the traditional placement of other psalms has been treated as secondary to the thematic consideration. Generally this has occurred when no valid internal reason could be seen for retaining the psalm only as a morning psalm or as an evening psalm. On Friday of year B/proper 17, for example, Psalm 17 is used as an evening psalm. Psalm 17 is usually listed as a morning psalm. There is, however, no apparent internal reason for this. Indeed, its plea that God "try by night" might more reasonably suggest an evening use. On Wednesday of Trinity week/year B, Psalms 14 and 53 are used. Both are often treated as evening psalms, yet Psalm 53 occurs as a morning psalm in other lectionaries, such as the Taize Office.

Such discussion, however, points out the basic ambiguity of language and expression that characterizes so much of the Psalter. It is this very ambiguity that allows us to see so much of our experience in the psalms. It is this very ambiguity that enables the psalms to teach us to pray. We see our own inner life through the emotional and spiritual lens of the psalms.

Learning to pray is perhaps the most difficult undertaking of the Christian life. True prayer never is achieved easily or quickly. On the path of Christian prayer, we inevitably turn aside on dead-end roads or become bogged down in some quagmire. The psalms, along with daily meditation upon God's word, are important companions and guides on our Christian journey.

> Our soul waits for the Lord;
>   he is our help and shield.
> Yea, our heart is glad in him,
>   because we trust in his holy name.
> Let thy steadfast love, O Lord, be upon us,
>   even as we hope in thee.
>   —33:20-22

Notes

1. Dietrich Bonhoeffer, *Psalms: The Prayer Book of the Bible*, trans. James H. Burtness (Minneapolis: Augsburg Publishing House, 1974), 11.
2. Ibid., 9-10.
3. Athanasius, *The Life of Antony and the Letter to Marcellinus*, trans. Robert C. Gregg (New York: Paulist Press, 1980), 108.
4. Ibid., 109.

4
AN INVITATION

This book is an invitation for every Christian to discover the daily practice of prayer and to hear the word of God in scripture through regular and planned meditation. This programmed sequence of scripture readings, called a daily lectionary, is the guide needed to get started on the daily practice of praising God through prayer and meditation.

This guide does not take the place of Sunday morning worship services. The vast majority of Christians will readily admit that Sunday morning is the principle time for worship. Sunday, the first day of the week, is the day Christians gather at church to celebrate the resurrection of our Lord Jesus Christ. We have certain expectations about what worship includes, expectations such as Bible-centered Sunday school lessons, preaching from the scripture, prayer, and singing. We consider the sacraments of baptism and the Lord's Supper to be an important, though maybe infrequent, part of our church services. Sunday, the Lord's day when the Lord's people gather around the Lord's table, is the necessary first act for a people committed to daily prayer.

This book is based on the assumption that many Christians long for some form of daily worship in addition to Sunday. The Sunday service is important and vital to the Christian life of faith. So, too, is a daily pattern of prayer and reading of scripture, which provides a different setting for prayer, praise, and attention to the voice of God. All relationships, including our relationship with God, require constant attention and regular attendance. Many Christians have discovered the need and desire to attend every day to their relationship with God by prayer and praise.

A Daily Lectionary

Jesus told his disciples to "ask," "seek," and "pray." Prayer has always been a chief activity of the church as a whole and of believers as individuals, whether it be prayers of supplication, intercession, praise, or thanksgiving. The apostle Paul, who had the example of his own Jewish background as well as the command of Christ as a guide, told his correspondents to "pray without ceasing." Readers of his letters through the years have considered unceasing prayer the goal toward which all should strive.

A Pattern for Daily Prayer

Though there may be many set hours for daily prayer, even as many as eight, morning and evening prayers are still the hinges around which daily prayer turns. In using this lectionary, a group of believers committed to daily prayer might covenant together to meet regularly for a full cycle, which would include both morning and evening prayer. The time of prayer should be centered on the two most important elements of the service: the appointed psalms and scripture lessons.

Morning is an appropriate time for giving thanks and praise for the resurrection of Christ. With the new light of day comes the hope of new life and new creation. Morning prayer should begin with an opening greeting, which may recall the theme of light, followed by a suitable morning hymn and an opening prayer. Two psalms are appointed in this lectionary for each day; the first is the morning psalm and the second is for evening. Following the opening prayer, the morning psalm for that day may be read or sung by the whole group. Silence for meditation normally follows the psalm, then, perhaps, a prayer that recaptures the movement of that psalm. The reading from scripture follows the psalm, and each group will have to make some decision about which lesson, or lessons, to use. Most groups will choose either the Old Testament reading or the Gospel reading; sometimes both will be read. After the reading, a period of silence should be allowed before a canticle or song is sung. After the singing, the community joins in prayers of thanksgiving, intercession, and petition. Ordinarily, it is best if these prayers are unstructured, though it is sometimes helpful for the leader of the service to bid prayer around certain themes. The service may then end with another hymn, a benediction, and the exchange of the peace.

This pattern of opening, psalm, scripture, canticle or song, prayers, and dismissal is useful for evening prayer, also. Evening prayer anticipates the day to come, as it also examines the day just past. The opening and the hymns should reflect the evening character of the prayer. At this service, it is appropriate to light candles as signs of Christ's light, which shines in the darkness.

Either the morning or evening service of prayer can include Holy Communion if this is desired. In such cases, the order of service should be shaped much like that of a Sunday morning pattern. The psalm, for instance, would come in between the lessons of scripture. In the morning, the service would begin with an opening (greeting, hymn, and prayer) followed by a reading of the Old Testament lesson, the psalm, then the Gospel lesson. The prayers would follow the Gospel lesson and the service of Communion would follow the prayers. In the evening of that day, the epistle lesson could be read. This pattern, which looks like the Sunday morning pattern, could be used without the service of Holy Communion, too, so that two lessons are read at one service and the third lesson is read at the other service.

The daily lectionary itself is arranged on a three-year cycle, thus the lessons are repeated every fourth year. The lessons are designed to correspond to the CCT Sunday Common Lectionary. Year A began with the first Sunday of Advent in 1983 and carried over into 1984. Year B began with the first Sunday in Advent 1984 and carried over into 1985. Year C began with the first Sunday of Advent 1985 and ran into 1986. After the three-year cycle is complete, it begins again. Therefore, year A will run from Advent 1986 to Advent 1987. Year B will run from Advent 1987 to Advent 1988. Year C will run from Advent 1988 to Advent 1989.

The lessons are dated from the Sunday that begins each week;

A Daily Lectionary

the lessons for Monday through Saturday of that week are listed after the Sunday lessons. Any lesson may be lengthened; some suggested lengthenings are indicated by parentheses. Sometimes more than one psalm is listed for either morning or evening, meaning that either or both may be used.

The lectionary incorporates some weeks that will not be necessary each year. This is because the date of Easter changes from year to year. Each year participants will skip some of the readings, as is indicated in the body of the lectionary.

Community or Individual Prayer

Already comparatively small groups, and sometimes whole congregations, throughout Christendom gather during the week for Bible study, prayer, sharing, and fellowship. For these groups, the move to a pattern of prayer suggested here and the use of this lectionary will be easy. This format for daily prayer can be a ten-minute service as comfortably as a thirty-minute one.

Christians meeting together for worship are the church, no matter how small the group, because "where two or three are gathered together," there the present Christ is also. The communal dimension of the Christian faith is always presupposed, and it is always assumed that daily prayer is a community activity. Indeed, as Thomas Hawkins has already suggested, neither the scripture nor prayer nor even faith itself belong to an individual, but are, rather, community property.

Nevertheless, there will always be some who cannot be present at the communal gatherings for daily prayer. In fact, this may be true for the majority of church members. Yet, those who pray individually are never alone, because they pray precisely as members of the church. This, then, will also be a useful resource for individuals who desire to stay "in community," because it allows the individual to hear the one spirit of God through the lessons from scripture.

It is the hope of the authors that this daily lectionary will

An Invitation

nurture a biblically literate community while facilitating a prayerful encounter with the word of God. In the long run, it is a deeper encounter with God that is the purpose of such a project. This goal is not restricted to denominational lines; it is intended that this work be useful ecumenically.

In a very real sense, we join in the communion of the saints through all ages and generations when we hear God's word and lift our voices in praise, thanksgiving, and petition for ourselves and others. This is our morning and evening sacrifice of ourselves, which we offer in union with Christ's one sacrifice for us, to the glory of the Father, and of the Son, and of the Holy Spirit.

PART II

5
YEAR A

Advent 1

Sunday	Morning Psalm: 122		Evening Psalm: 145
	Isa. 2:1-5	Matt. 24:36-44	Rom. 13:11-14
Monday	Morning Psalm: 97		Evening Psalm: 25
	Isa. 2:6-11	Matt. 25:1-13	Acts 1:6-11
Tuesday	Morning Psalm: 75		Evening Psalm: 62
	Isa. 2:12-22	Matt. 25:14-30	1 Thess. 5:1-11
Wednesday	Morning Psalm: 90		Evening Psalm: 94
	Isa. 3:8-15	Matt. 25:31-46	2 Pet. 3:8-18
Thursday	Morning Psalm: 76		Evening Psalm: 43
	Isa. 4:2-6	John 1:6-13	Acts 10:9-16
Friday	Morning Psalm: 80		Evening Psalm: 40
	Isa. 5:1-7	John 1:19-28	Rev. 5:1-10
Saturday	Morning Psalm: 28		Evening Psalm: 49
	Isa. 5:8-12, 18-23	John 1:29-42	Rom. 3:21-31

Advent 2

Sunday	Morning Psalm: 72		Evening Psalm: 7
	Isa. 11:1-10	Matt. 3:1-12	Rom. 15:4-13
Monday	Morning Psalm: 109		Evening Psalm: 12
	Isa. 5:13-17, 24-25	John 3:22-36	Acts 10:34-43
Tuesday	Morning Psalm: 119:65-88		Evening Psalm: 119:89-120
	Isa. 6:1-13	John 5:30-47	Rev. 22:16-20
Wednesday	Morning Psalm: 61		Evening Psalm: 31
	Isa. 7:1-9	Matt. 11:1-6	Gal. 6:1-10
Thursday	Morning Psalm: 86		Evening Psalm: 127
	Isa. 7:10-25	Matt. 11:7-15	Heb. 10:32-39
Friday	Morning Psalm: 58		Evening Psalm: 25
	Isa. 8:1-15	Matt. 11:16-24	1 Thess. 5:1-11
Saturday	Morning Psalm: 42		Evening Psalm: 33
	Isa. 8:16-9:1	Matt. 17:9-13	Rom. 13:8-14

A Daily Lectionary

Advent 3

Sunday	Morning Psalm: 146 Isa. 35:1-10	Matt. 11:2-11	Evening Psalm: 30 James 5:7-10
Monday	Morning Psalm: 150 Isa. 9:1-7	Matt. 21:23-32	Evening Psalm: 21 Heb. 12:18-29
Tuesday	Morning Psalm: 79 Isa. 9:8-17	Matt. 18:1-6	Evening Psalm: 96 2 Thess. 2:1-3, 13-17
Wednesday	Morning Psalm: 99 Isa. 9:18-10:4	John 10:31-42	Evening Psalm: 82 Heb. 10:19-25
Thursday	Morning Psalm: 32 Isa. 10:5-19	John 4:1-15	Evening Psalm: 53 Rom. 4:1-8
Friday	Morning Psalm: 78:1-31 Isa. 10:20-27	John 4:16-30	Evening Psalm: 87 Rom. 4:9-15
Saturday	Morning Psalm: 132 Isa. 11:1-9	Matt. 1:1-17	Evening Psalm: 78:32-72 Rom. 4:16-25

Advent 4*

Sunday	Morning Psalm: 24 Isa. 7:10-16	Matt. 1:18-25	Evening Psalm: 100 Rom. 5:1-7
Monday	Morning Psalm: 2 Isa. 11:10-16	John 1:14-18	Evening Psalm: 20 Rev. 12:1-9
Tuesday	Morning Psalm: 140 Isa. 13:6-13	John 3:1-8	Evening Psalm: 114 Rev. 12:10-17
Wednesday	Morning Psalm: 118 Isa. 28:9-22	John 3:9-21	Evening Psalm: 8 Heb. 2:1-9
Thursday	Morning Psalm: 66 Isa. 29:13-24	John 5:19-29	Evening Psalm: 64 Titus 1:1-16
Friday	Morning Psalm: 15 Isa. 33:17-22	John 6:27-34	Evening Psalm: 48 Titus 2:1-10
Saturday	Morning Psalm: 98 Isa. 59:15b-21	John 6:35-40	Evening Psalm: 113 Titus 2:11-3:7

Christmas Eve

Morning Psalm: 96 Isa. 9:2-7	Luke 1:1-20	Evening Psalm: 2 Titus 2:11-14

*Skip to Christmas Eve lesson on Christmas Eve.

Year A

Christmas Day
    Morning Psalm: 110   Evening Psalm: 85
    Isa. 62:6-7, 10-12 or   Luke 2:8-20 or   Titus 3:4-7 or
    Isa. 52:7-10   John 1:1-14   Heb. 1:1-12

Dec. 26   Morning Psalm: 107:1-25   Evening Psalm: 107:26-45
           2 Chron. 24:17-22   Acts 7:55-8:8   Acts 6:1-7

Dec. 27   Morning Psalm: 104:1-23   Evening Psalm: 104:24-35, 41
           Prov. 8:22-30   John 13:2-20   1 John 1:1-9

Dec. 28   Morning Psalm: 77   Evening Psalm: 57
           Jer. 31:15-17   Matt. 2:13-18   Rev. 21:1-7

Dec. 29   Morning Psalm: 18:1-20   Evening Psalm: 18:21-50
           Isa. 41:14-20   John 4:7-15   Rev. 1:1-8

Dec. 30   Morning Psalm: 37:1-22   Evening Psalm: 37:23-40
           Isa. 25:1-9   John 7:53-8:11   3 John 1-15

Dec. 31   Morning Psalm: 46   Evening Psalm: 139:1-18(19-24)
           Isa. 26:1-6   John 8:12-19   2 Cor. 5:16-6:2

1st Sunday after Christmas*
    Morning Psalm: 111   Evening Psalm: 95
    Isa. 63:7-9   Matt. 2:13-15, 19-23   Heb. 2:10-18

Jan. 1   Morning Psalm: 106:1-23   Evening Psalm: 106:24-48
           Deut. 8:1-10   Matt. 25:31-46   Rev. 21:1-6a

Jan. 2   Morning Psalm: 63   Evening Psalm: 1
           2 Kings 4:42-44   John 6:35-42   Eph. 4:1-16

Jan. 3   Morning Psalm: 121   Evening Psalm: 68
           Isa. 49:8-13   John 6:41-51   Eph. 4:17-32

Jan. 4   Morning Psalm: 70   Evening Psalm: 135
           Exod. 3:1-15   John 14:6-14   Heb. 11:23-31

Jan. 5   Morning Psalm: 55   Evening Psalm: 105
           Deut. 7:6-11   John 15:1-16   1 John 5:6-12

2nd Sunday after Christmas**
    Morning Psalm: 66   Evening Psalm: 117
    Jer. 31:7-14   John 1:1-18   Eph. 1:3-6, 15-18

*When a Sunday lesson coincides with a dated lesson, the Sunday lesson should be read.

**If this is Epiphany, skip to Epiphany reading. This lesson is not read during years in which only one Sunday falls between Christmas and Epiphany.

A Daily Lectionary

Epiphany	Morning Psalm: 27	Evening Psalm: 112
	Isa. 60:1-6	Matt. 2:1-12	Eph. 3:1-12
Jan. 7	Morning Psalm: 4	Evening Psalm: 44
	Isa. 52:3-6	Matt. 12:14-21	Rev. 2:1-7
Jan. 8	Morning Psalm: 119:1-24	Evening Psalm: 119:25-56
	Isa. 60:1-7	John 4:46-54	Rev. 21:22-27
Jan. 9	Morning Psalm: 119:57-72	Evening Psalm: 119:73-96
	Isa. 63:1-5	John 5:1-18	Rev. 2:8-17
Jan. 10	Morning Psalm: 119:97-120	Evening Psalm: 119:121-144
	Jer. 23:1-8	John 6:1-14	Rom. 3:21-26
Jan. 11	Morning Psalm: 103	Evening Psalm: 119:145-176
	Isa. 55:3-9	John 6:15-27	Rev. 3:1-6
Jan. 12	Morning Psalm: 128	Evening Psalm: 60
	Gen. 49:1-2, 8-12	John 6:52-71	Col. 3:18-46

1st Sunday after Epiphany*

Sunday	Morning Psalm: 148	Evening Psalm: 29
	Isa. 42:1-9	Matt. 3:13-17	Acts 10:34-43
Monday	Morning Psalm: 45	Evening Psalm: 102
	Isa. 40:1-11	John 2:1-12	Heb. 1:1-14
Tuesday	Morning Psalm: 69	Evening Psalm: 19
	Isa. 40:12-23	John 2:13-22	Heb. 2:1-10
Wednesday	Morning Psalm: 89:1-33	Evening Psalm: 89:34-52
	Isa. 40:25-31	John 2:23-3:15	Acts 18:5-10
Thursday	Morning Psalm: 67	Evening Psalm: 138
	Isa. 41:1-16	John 4:31-45	1 Tim. 2:1-7
Friday	Morning Psalm: 124	Evening Psalm: 115
	Isa. 41:17-29	Matt. 10:34-42	Rom. 8:1-8
Saturday	Morning Psalm: 116	Evening Psalm: 108
	Isa. 43:1-13	Matt. 11:25-30	Eph. 3:14-21

*Begin this week of readings on the first Sunday after Epiphany, skipping any dated material necessary.

Year A

2nd Sunday after Epiphany

Sunday	Morning Psalm: 63		Evening Psalm: 136
	Isa. 49:1-7	John 1:29-34	1 Cor. 1:1-9
Monday	Morning Psalm: 59		Evening Psalm: 141
	Isa. 43:14-44:5	Luke 3:15-22	1 Cor. 1:10-17
Tuesday	Morning Psalm: 47		Evening Psalm: 4
	Isa. 44:6-8, 21-23	Luke 7:18-23	1 Cor. 1:18-25
Wednesday	Morning Psalm: 5		Evening Psalm: 65
	Isa. 44:9-20	Matt. 8:18-27	1 Cor. 1:26-31
Thursday	Morning Psalm: 3		Evening Psalm: 73
	Isa. 44:24-45:7	John 1:43-51	1 Cor. 2:1-9
Friday	Morning Psalm: 149		Evening Psalm: 36
	Isa. 45:5-17	Luke 5:1-11	1 Cor. 2:10-16
Saturday	Morning Psalm: 54		Evening Psalm: 91
	Isa. 45:18-25	Matt. 4:1-11	1 Cor. 3:1-9

3rd Sunday after Epiphany

Sunday	Morning Psalm: 71		Evening Psalm: 134
	Isa. 9:1-4	Matt. 4:12-23	1 Cor. 1:10-17
Monday	Morning Psalm: 52		Evening Psalm: 6
	Isa. 46:1-13	Luke 3:1-14	1 Cor. 3:10-17
Tuesday	Morning Psalm: 88		Evening Psalm: 2
	Isa. 47:1-15	Luke 3:15-22	1 Cor. 3:18-23
Wednesday	Morning Psalm: 68:1-18		Evening Psalm: 68:19-35
	Isa. 48:1-11	Luke 4:1-13	1 Cor. 4:1-5
Thursday	Morning Psalm: 120		Evening Psalm: 38
	Isa. 48:12-21	Luke 4:14-30	1 Cor. 4:6-13
Friday	Morning Psalm: 22		Evening Psalm: 36
	Isa. 49:1-12	Luke 4:31-37	1 Cor. 4:14-21
Saturday	Morning Psalm: 131		Evening Psalm: 56
	Isa. 49:13-23	Luke 4:38-44	1 Cor. 5:1-5

A Daily Lectionary

4th Sunday after Epiphany*

Sunday	Morning Psalm: 1 Mic. 6:1-8	Matt. 5:1-12	Evening Psalm: 128 1 Cor. 1:18-31
Monday	Morning Psalm: 143 Isa. 50:1-11	Luke 5:1-11	Evening Psalm: 35 1 Cor. 5:6-13
Tuesday	Morning Psalm: 123 Isa. 51:1-8	Luke 5:12-16	Evening Psalm: 17 1 Cor. 6:1-8
Wednesday	Morning Psalm: 74 Isa. 51:9-16	Luke 5:27-39	Evening Psalm: 26 1 Cor. 6:9-11
Thursday	Morning Psalm: 9 Isa. 51:17-23	Luke 6:1-11	Evening Psalm: 101 1 Cor. 6:12-20
Friday	Morning Psalm: 93 Isa. 52:1-12	Luke 6:12-26	Evening Psalm: 11 1 Cor. 7:1-7
Saturday	Morning Psalm: 39 Isa. 54:1-17	Luke 6:27-38	Evening Psalm: 10 1 Cor. 7:8-11

5th Sunday after Epiphany*

Sunday	Morning Psalm: 112 Isa. 58:3-9a	Matt. 5:13-16	Evening Psalm: 148 1 Cor. 2:1-11
Monday	Morning Psalm: 133 Isa. 56:1-8	Luke 6:39-49	Evening Psalm: 10 1 Cor. 7:12-16
Tuesday	Morning Psalm: 32 Isa. 57:3-13	Luke 7:1-17	Evening Psalm: 13 1 Cor. 7:17-24
Wednesday	Morning Psalm: 85 Isa. 57:14-21	Luke 7:18-35	Evening Psalm: 140 1 Cor. 7:25-31
Thursday	Morning Psalm: 125 Isa. 59:1-15a	Luke 7:36-50	Evening Psalm: 14 1 Cor. 7:32-40
Friday	Morning Psalm: 7 Isa. 59:15b-21	Luke 8:1-15	Evening Psalm: 126 1 Cor. 8:1-6
Saturday	Morning Psalm: 34 Isa. 60:1-17	Luke 8:16-25	Evening Psalm: 84 1 Cor. 8:7-13

*If this is last Sunday after Epiphany, skip to Transfiguration Sunday.

Year A

Proper 1 (*6th Sunday after Epiphany*)*

Sunday	Morning Psalm: 119:1-16		Evening Psalm: 36
	Deut. 30:15-20	Matt. 5:17-26	1 Cor. 3:1-9
Monday	Morning Psalm: 23		Evening Psalm: 16
	Isa. 61:1-9	Luke 8:26-39	1 Cor. 9:1-12a
Tuesday	Morning Psalm: 124		Evening Psalm: 72
	Isa. 61:10-62:5	Luke 8:40-56	1 Cor. 9:12b-18
Wednesday	Morning Psalm: 81		Evening Psalm: 122
	Isa. 62:6-12	Luke 9:1-17	1 Cor. 9:19-27
Thursday	Morning Psalm: 98		Evening Psalm: 33
	Isa. 63:1-6	Luke 9:18-27	1 Cor. 10:1-13
Friday	Morning Psalm: 17		Evening Psalm: 100
	Isa. 63:7-14	Luke 9:28-36	1 Cor. 10:14-22
Saturday	Morning Psalm: 144		Evening Psalm: 51
	Isa. 63:15-64:9	Luke 9:37-50	1 Cor. 10:23-11:1

Proper 2 (*7th Sunday after Epiphany*)*

Sunday	Morning Psalm: 147		Evening Psalm: 103
	Isa. 49:8-13	Matt. 5:27-37	1 Cor. 3:10-11, 16-23
Monday	Morning Psalm: 50		Evening Psalm: 141
	Isa. 65:1-12	Luke 9:51-62	1 Cor. 11:2-10
Tuesday	Morning Psalm: 92		Evening Psalm: 94
	Isa. 65:17-25	Luke 10:1-17	1 Cor. 11:11-16
Wednesday	Morning Psalm: 34		Evening Psalm: 40
	Isa. 66:1-6	Luke 10:17-24	1 Cor. 11:17-26
Thursday	Morning Psalm: 87		Evening Psalm: 137
	Isa. 66:7-14	Luke 10:25-37	1 Cor. 11:27-34
Friday	Morning Psalm: 27		Evening Psalm: 133
	Lev. 8:1-13, 30-36	Luke 10:38-42	1 Cor. 12:1-6
Saturday	Morning Psalm: 83		Evening Psalm: 63:24-35
	Lev. 16:1-19	Matt. 6:1-6, 16-18	1 Cor. 12:7-13

If this is last Sunday after Epiphany, skip to Transfiguration Sunday.

A Daily Lectionary

Proper 3 (*8th Sunday after Epiphany*)*

Sunday	Morning Psalm: 146		Evening Psalm: 68:1-23
	Lev. 19:1-2, 9-18	Matt. 5:38-48	1 Cor. 4:1-5
Monday	Morning Psalm: 80		Evening Psalm: 85
	Lev. 16:20-34	Matt. 6:7-15	1 Cor. 12:14-26
Tuesday	Morning Psalm: 12		Evening Psalm: 15
	Lev. 19:26-37	Matt. 6:19-24	1 Cor. 12:27-31
Wednesday	Morning Psalm: 81		Evening Psalm: 147
	Lev. 23:1-22	Matt. 6:25-34	Gal. 1:1-10
Thursday	Morning Psalm: 106:1-23		Evening Psalm: 106:24-48
	Lev. 23:23-44	Matt. 7:1-12	Gal. 1:11-17
Friday	Morning Psalm: 125		Evening Psalm: 9
	Lev. 25:1-17	Matt. 7:13-21	Gal. 1:18-24
Saturday	Morning Psalm: 1		Evening Psalm: 119:89-112
	Deut. 6:1-9	John 12:24-32	Heb. 12:18-29

Transfiguration Sunday (*Last Sunday after Epiphany*)

Sunday	Morning Psalm: 2		Evening Psalm: 118
	Exod. 24:12-18	Matt. 17:1-9	2 Pet. 1:16-21
Monday	Morning Psalm: 82		Evening Psalm: 146
	Amos 5:6-15	Matt. 17:9-13	Gal. 2:1-10
Tuesday	Morning Psalm: 130		Evening Psalm: 126
	Jon. 3:1-4:11	Matt. 7:21-29	Gal. 2:11-21

Ash Wednesday

	Morning Psalm: 51		Evening Psalm: 38
	Joel 2:1-2, 12-17a	Matt. 6:1-6, 16-21	2 Cor. 5:20b-6:10
Thursday	Morning Psalm: 37:1-20		Evening Psalm: 37:21-40
	Lev. 25:35-55	Matt. 8:1-13	Gal. 3:1-5
Friday	Morning Psalm: 106:1-27		Evening Psalm: 106:28-48
	Lev. 26:1-20	Matt. 8:14-22	Gal. 3:6-14
Saturday	Morning Psalm: 74		Evening Psalm: 65
	Lev. 26:27-42	Matt. 8:23-34	Gal. 3:15-20

**If this is last Sunday after Epiphany, skip to Transfiguration Sunday.*

Year A

Lent 1

Sunday	Morning Psalm: 25 Gen. 2:4b-9, 15-17, 25, 3:1-7	Matt. 4:1-11	Evening Psalm: 91 Rom. 5:12-19
Monday	Morning Psalm: 135 Jer. 10:1-10	Matt. 9:1-9	Evening Psalm: 115 Gal. 3:21-29
Tuesday	Morning Psalm: 70 Jer. 10:11-16, 23-25	Matt. 9:10-17	Evening Psalm: 72 Gal. 4:1-7
Wednesday	Morning Psalm: 78:1-31 Deut. 8:1-10	Matt. 9:18-26	Evening Psalm: 78:32-72 Gal. 4:8-14
Thursday	Morning Psalm: 107:1-22 Deut. 8:11-20	Matt. 9:27-38	Evening Psalm: 107:23-43 Gal. 4:15-20
Friday	Morning Psalm: 80 Deut. 9:4-12	Matt. 10:1-15	Evening Psalm: 16 Gal. 4:21-31
Saturday	Morning Psalm: 31 Deut. 9:13-21	Matt. 10:16-23	Evening Psalm: 85 Gal. 5:1-6

Lent 2

Sunday	Morning Psalm: 105 Gen. 12:1-8	John 3:1-17	Evening Psalm: 32 Rom. 4:1-17
Monday	Morning Psalm: 106:1-23 Deut. 9:23-10:5	Matt. 10:24-33	Evening Psalm: 27 Gal. 5:7-12
Tuesday	Morning Psalm: 63 Deut. 10:12-22	Matt. 10:34-42	Evening Psalm: 15 Gal. 5:13-18
Wednesday	Morning Psalm: 143 Isa. 58:1-5	Matt. 11:1-15	Evening Psalm: 112 Gal. 5:19-26
Thursday	Morning Psalm: 12 Isa. 58:6-14	Matt. 11:16-30	Evening Psalm: 133 Gal. 6:1-6
Friday	Morning Psalm: 62 Ezek. 28:1-10	John 6:1-15	Evening Psalm: 20 Gal. 6:7-18
Saturday	Morning Psalm: 58 Ezek. 28:11-19	John 6:16-27	Evening Psalm: 52 2 Cor. 1:1-11

A Daily Lectionary

Lent 3

Sunday	Morning Psalm: 19		Evening Psalm: 81
	Exod. 17:3-7	John 4:5-26 (or 42)	Rom. 5:1-11
Monday	Morning Psalm: 119:1-24		Evening Psalm: 119:25-56
	Ezek. 30:1-9	John 6:27-40	2 Cor. 1:12-22
Tuesday	Morning Psalm: 119:56-80		Evening Psalm: 119:81-104
	Ezek. 31:1-11	John 6:41-51	2 Cor. 1:23-2:17
Wednesday	Morning Psalm: 119:105-128		Evening Psalm: 119:129-152
	Ezek. 33:1-11	John 6:52-59	2 Cor. 3:1-18
Thursday	Morning Psalm: 119:153-176		Evening Psalm: 6
	Ezek. 33:12-20	John 6:60-71	2 Cor. 4:1-6
Friday	Morning Psalm: 3		Evening Psalm: 116
	Ezek. 33:21-33	John 7:1-13	2 Cor. 4:7-15
Saturday	Morning Psalm: 23		Evening Psalm: 25
	Ezek. 34:1-16	John 7:14-36	2 Cor. 4:16-5:5

Lent 4

Sunday	Morning Psalm: 34		Evening Psalm: 23
	1 Sam. 16:1-13	John 9:1-41	Eph. 5:8-14
Monday	Morning Psalm: 100		Evening Psalm: 65
	Ezek. 34:17-31	John 7:37-52	2 Cor. 5:6-15
Tuesday	Morning Psalm: 106:1-23		Evening Psalm: 106:24-48
	Ezek. 36:8-21	John 8:1-11	2 Cor. 5:16-21
Wednesday	Morning Psalm: 126		Evening Psalm: 51
	Ezek. 36:22-32	John 8:12-20	2 Cor. 6:1-13
Thursday	Morning Psalm: 47		Evening Psalm: 132
	Ezek. 37:21b-28	John 8:21-32	2 Cor. 10:1-6
Friday	Morning Psalm: 38		Evening Psalm: 36
	Ezek. 39:1-10	John 8:33-47	2 Cor. 10:7-18
Saturday	Morning Psalm: 80		Evening Psalm: 85
	Ezek. 39:21-29	John 8:47-59	2 Cor. 11:1-6

Year A

Lent 5

Sunday	Morning Psalm: 51 Ezek. 37:1-14	John 11:1-45	Evening Psalm: 104 Rom. 8:6-11
Monday	Morning Psalm: 146 Ezek. 43:1-12	John 9:1-17	Evening Psalm: 47 2 Cor. 11:7-15
Tuesday	Morning Psalm: 103 Ezek. 47:1-12	John 9:18-41	Evening Psalm: 46 2 Cor. 11:16-29
Wednesday	Morning Psalm: 23 Dan. 12:1-13	John 10:1-18	Evening Psalm: 100 2 Cor. 11:30-12:6
Thursday	Morning Psalm: 2 Ezek. 3:4-11	John 10:19-42	Evening Psalm: 92 2 Cor. 12:7-11
Friday	Morning Psalm: 5 Jer. 31:16-25	John 11:1-27	Evening Psalm: 94 2 Cor. 12:12-21
Saturday	Morning Psalm: 148 Jer. 31:27-37	John 11:28-44	Evening Psalm: 19 2 Cor. 13:1-14

Holy Week
Passion/Palm Sunday

	Morning Psalm: 24 Isa. 50:4-9a	Matt. 26:14-27:66 or Matt. 21:1-11	Evening Psalm: 118:19-29 Phil. 2:5-11
Monday	Morning Psalm: 69:1-23 Isa. 42:1-9	John 12:1-11	Evening Psalm: 36 Heb. 9:11-15
Tuesday	Morning Psalm: 71 Isa. 49:1-7	John 12:20-36	Evening Psalm: 110 1 Cor. 1:18-31
Wednesday	Morning Psalm: 41 Isa. 50:4-9a	John 13:21-30	Evening Psalm: 55 Heb. 12:1-3

Maundy Thursday

Morning Psalm: 102 Exod. 12:1-14	John 13:1-15	Evening Psalm: 142 1 Cor. 11:23-26

Good Friday

Morning Psalm: 54 Isa. 52:13-53:12	John 18:1-19:42 or 19:17-30	Evening Psalm: 22 Heb. 4:14-16, 5:7-9

Holy Saturday

Morning Psalm: 88 Exod. 14:10-15:18	Matt. 28:1-10	Evening Psalm: 27 Rom. 6:3-11

A Daily Lectionary

Easter Sunday

Sunday	Morning Psalm: 150 Acts 10:34-43 or Jer. 31:1-6	John 20:1-18 or Matt. 28:1-10	Evening Psalm: 118:14-24 Col. 3:1-4 or Acts 10:34-43
Monday	Morning Psalm: 93 Jon. 2:1-9	Luke 23:5b-24:11	Evening Psalm: 66 1 Cor. 15:1-11
Tuesday	Morning Psalm: 149 Isa. 30:18-26	Luke 24:12-27	Evening Psalm: 111 1 Cor. 15:12-28
Wednesday	Morning Psalm: 97 Mic. 7:7-15	Luke 24:28-35	Evening Psalm: 99 1 Cor. 15:30-41
Thursday	Morning Psalm: 147 Ezek. 37:1-14	Luke 24:36-44	Evening Psalm: 40 1 Cor. 15:41-50
Friday	Morning Psalm: 136 Isa. 25:1-9	Luke 24:45-53	Evening Psalm: 144 1 Cor. 15:51-58
Saturday	Morning Psalm: 145 Isa. 43:8-13	John 20:1-18	Evening Psalm: 138 2 Cor. 4:16-5:10

Easter 2

Sunday	Morning Psalm: 133 Acts 2:14a, 22-32	John 20:19-31	Evening Psalm: 117 1 Pet. 1:3-9
Monday	Morning Psalm: 132 Dan. 1:1-21	John 21:1-14	Evening Psalm: 28 1 Pet. 1:1-2, 10-12
Tuesday	Morning Psalm: 12 Dan. 2:1-16	John 21:15-19	Evening Psalm: 145 1 Pet. 1:13-21
Wednesday	Morning Psalm: 43 Dan. 2:17-30	John 21:20-25	Evening Psalm: 113 1 Pet. 1:22-2:3
Thursday	Morning Psalm: 82 Dan. 2:31-49	John 14:1-7	Evening Psalm: 60 1 Pet. 2:4-10
Friday	Morning Psalm: 26 Dan. 3:1-18	John 14:8-17	Evening Psalm: 39 1 Pet. 2:11-12
Saturday	Morning Psalm: 140 Dan. 3:19-30	John 14:18-24	Evening Psalm: 34 1 Pet. 2:13-17

Year A

Easter 3

Sunday	Morning Psalm: 33 Acts 2:14a, 36-41	Luke 24:13-35	Evening Psalm: 4 1 Pet. 1:17-23
Monday	Morning Psalm: 49 Dan. 4:1-18	John 15:1-11	Evening Psalm: 14 1 Pet. 2:18-25
Tuesday	Morning Psalm: 83 Dan. 4:19-27	John 15:12-27	Evening Psalm: 35 1 Pet. 3:1-7
Wednesday	Morning Psalm: 131 Dan. 4:28-37	John 16:1-11	Evening Psalm: 141 1 Pet. 3:8-12
Thursday	Morning Psalm: 73 Dan. 5:1-12	John 17:1-11	Evening Psalm: 101 1 Pet. 3:13-17
Friday	Morning Psalm: 64 Dan. 5:13-30	John 17:12-19	Evening Psalm: 53 1 Pet. 3:18-22
Saturday	Morning Psalm: 109 Dan. 6:1-15	John 17:20-26	Evening Psalm: 86 1 Pet. 4:1-6

Easter 4

Sunday	Morning Psalm: 100 Acts 2:42-47	John 10:1-10	Evening Psalm: 23 1 Pet. 2:19-25
Monday	Morning Psalm: 54 Dan. 6:16-28	Matt. 12:1-8	Evening Psalm: 102 1 Pet. 4:7-11
Tuesday	Morning Psalm: 108 Jer. 30:10-17	Matt. 12:9-21	Evening Psalm: 40 1 Pet. 4:12-16
Wednesday	Morning Psalm: 125 Jer. 30:18-22	Matt. 12:22-32	Evening Psalm: 120 1 Pet. 4:17-19
Thursday	Morning Psalm: 30 Jer. 31:1-14	Matt. 12:33-42	Evening Psalm: 77 1 Pet. 5:1-5
Friday	Morning Psalm: 17 Jer. 31:15-22	Matt. 12:43-50	Evening Psalm: 44 1 Pet. 5:6-14
Saturday	Morning Psalm: 92 Jer. 31:23-25	Matt. 13:1-9	Evening Psalm: 48 1 Cor. 13:1-7

A Daily Lectionary

Easter 5

Sunday	Morning Psalm: 22:25-31		Evening Psalm: 90
	Acts 7:55-60	John 14:1-14	1 Pet. 2:2-10
Monday	Morning Psalm: 9		Evening Psalm: 56
	Jer. 32:1-15	Matt. 13:10-17	1 Cor. 13:8-13
Tuesday	Morning Psalm: 68		Evening Psalm: 21
	Jer. 32:16-25	Matt. 13:18-24	1 Cor. 14:1-12
Wednesday	Morning Psalm: 114		Evening Psalm: 79
	Jer. 32:36-44	Matt. 13:31-35	1 Cor. 14:13-25
Thursday	Morning Psalm: 75		Evening Psalm: 50
	Jer. 33:1-13	Matt. 13:36-43	1 Cor. 14:26-32
Friday	Morning Psalm: 66		Evening Psalm: 124
	Deut. 31:30-32:14	Matt. 13:44-52	1 Cor. 14:33-39
Saturday	Morning Psalm: 129		Evening Psalm: 76
	Deut. 32:34-43	Matt. 13:53-58	1 Cor. 15:1-11

Easter 6

Sunday	Morning Psalm: 98		Evening Psalm: 134
	Acts 17:22-31	John 14:15-21	1 Pet. 3:13-22
Monday	Morning Psalm: 78:1-31		Evening Psalm: 78:32-72
	Deut. 8:1-10	John 14:22-31	1 Cor. 15:12-19
Tuesday	Morning Psalm: 128		Evening Psalm: 127
	Deut. 8:11-20	Matt. 28:1-15	1 Cor. 15:20-28
Wednesday	Morning Psalm: 130		Evening Psalm: 8
	Deut. 19:1-7	Matt. 28:16-20	Eph. 1:1-10

Ascension Day

	Morning Psalm: 96		Evening Psalm: 29
	Acts 1:1-11	Luke 24:46-53 or	Eph. 1:15-23
		Mark 16:9-16, 19-20	
Friday	Morning Psalm: 10		Evening Psalm: 7
	Ezek. 1:28-3:3	Matt. 14:1-12	1 Cor. 15:29-34
Saturday	Morning Psalm: 11		Evening Psalm: 139
	Ezek. 3:4-17	Matt. 14:13-21	1 Cor. 15:35-44

Year A

Easter 7

Sunday	Morning Psalm: 1		Evening Psalm: 121
	Acts 1:6-14	John 17:1-11	1 Pet. 4:12-14, 5:6-11
Monday	Morning Psalm: 42		Evening Psalm: 13
	Ezek. 3:16-27	Matt. 14:22-36	1 Cor. 15:45-58
Tuesday	Morning Psalm: 59		Evening Psalm: 61
	Ezek. 4:1-17	Matt. 15:1-20	1 Cor. 16:1-9
Wednesday	Morning Psalm: 123		Evening Psalm: 130
	Ezek. 7:10-15, 23b-27	Matt. 15:21-28	1 Cor. 16:10-24
Thursday	Morning Psalm: 122		Evening Psalm: 87
	Ezek. 11:14-25	Matt. 15:29-39	Acts 1:1-8
Friday	Morning Psalm: 57		Evening Psalm: 84
	Ezek. 18:1-4, 19-32	John 16:12-24	Acts 1:9-14
Saturday	Morning Psalm: 45		Evening Psalm: 85
	Isa. 11:1-9	John 16:25-31	Acts 1:15-26

Pentecost Sunday

Sunday	Morning Psalm: 104:1-18		Evening Psalm: 104:19-35
	Acts 2:1-21 or	John 20:19-23 or	1 Cor. 12:3b-13 or
	Isa. 44:1-8	John 7:37-39	Acts 2:1-21
Monday	Morning Psalm: 103		Evening Psalm: 139
	Gen. 2:4b-17	John 20:19-31	Acts 2:1-13
Tuesday	Morning Psalm: 106:1-12		Evening Psalm: 106:24-48
	Num. 11:16-25	Matt. 16:1-12	Acts 2:14-21
Wednesday	Morning Psalm: 78:1-31		Evening Psalm: 78:32-72
	Deut. 4:1-14	Matt. 16:13-20	Acts 2:22-28
Thursday	Morning Psalm: 116		Evening Psalm: 115
	Deut. 4:15-31	Matt. 16:21-28	Acts 2:29-36
Friday	Morning Psalm: 2		Evening Psalm: 99
	Deut. 6:1-15	Matt. 17:1-13	Acts 2:37-42
Saturday	Morning Psalm: 89:1-25		Evening Psalm: 89:26-52
	Job 38:1-11	Matt. 17:14-21	Acts 2:43-47

A Daily Lectionary

Trinity Sunday

Sunday	Morning Psalm: 150		Evening Psalm: 111
	Deut. 4:32-40	Matt. 28:16-20	2 Cor. 13:5-14
Monday	Morning Psalm: 148		Evening Psalm: 8
	Gen. 1:1-2:3	Matt. 17:22-27	Philem. 1-14
Tuesday	Morning Psalm: 131		Evening Psalm: 19
	Gen. 2:4-25	Matt. 18:1-9	Philem. 15-25
Wednesday	Morning Psalm: 34		Evening Psalm: 51
	Gen. 3:1-24	Matt. 18:10-20	Rom. 1:1-15
Thursday	Morning Psalm: 109		Evening Psalm: 130
	Gen. 4:1-16	Matt. 18:21-35	Rom. 1:16-25
Friday	Morning Psalm: 5		Evening Psalm: 49
	Gen. 4:17-26	Matt. 19:1-12	Rom. 1:26-32
Saturday	Morning Psalm: 119:1-24		Evening Psalm: 119:25-48
	Gen. 6:1-8	Matt. 19:13-22	Rom. 2:1-11

Proper 4 (*Sunday between May 29 and June 4 if after Trinity Sunday*)*

Sunday	Morning Psalm: 105:1-22		Evening Psalm: 105:23-45
	Gen. 12:1-9	Matt. 7:21-29	Rom. 3:21-28
Monday	Morning Psalm: 50		Evening Psalm: 62
	Gen. 9:4-22	Matt. 19:23-30	Rom. 2:12-16
Tuesday	Morning Psalm: 119:97-120		Evening Psalm: 119:121-152
	Gen. 7:1-10	Matt. 20:1-16	Rom. 2:17-24
Wednesday	Morning Psalm: 97		Evening Psalm: 114
	Gen. 7:11-24	Matt. 20:17-28	Rom. 2:25-26
Thursday	Morning Psalm: 10		Evening Psalm: 14
	Gen. 7:11-24	Matt. 20:29-34	Rom. 2:27-3:18
Friday	Morning Psalm: 118:1-14		Evening Psalm: 118:15-29
	Gen. 9:1-17	Matt. 21:1-11	Rom. 3:19-31
Saturday	Morning Psalm: 144		Evening Psalm: 32
	Gen. 9:18-29	Matt: 21:12-22	Rom. 4:1-12

If the Sunday between May 24 and 28 follows Trinity Sunday, go back to Proper 3.

Year A

Proper 5 (*Sunday between June 5 and 11 if after Trinity Sunday*)

Sunday	Morning Psalm: 40		Evening Psalm: 66
	Gen. 22:1-18	Matt. 9:9-13	Rom. 4:13-18
Monday	Morning Psalm: 119:49-72		Evening Psalm: 119:73-96
	Gen. 11:1-9	Matt. 21:23-32	Rom. 4:19-25
Tuesday	Morning Psalm: 80		Evening Psalm: 121
	Gen. 11:27-12:8	Matt. 21:33-46	Rom. 5:1-5
Wednesday	Morning Psalm: 38		Evening Psalm: 113
	Gen. 12:9-13:1	Matt. 22:1-14	Rom. 5:6-11
Thursday	Morning Psalm: 133		Evening Psalm: 112
	Gen. 13:2-18	Matt. 22:15-22	Rom. 5:12-21
Friday	Morning Psalm: 119:153-176		Evening Psalm: 110
	Gen. 14:(1-7) 8-24	Matt. 22:23-40	Rom. 6:1-11
Saturday	Morning Psalm: 147		Evening Psalm: 15
	Gen. 15:1-21	Matt. 22:41-46	Rom. 6:12-19

Proper 6 (*Sunday between June 12 and 18 if after Trinity Sunday*)

Sunday	Morning Psalm: 100		Evening Psalm: 127
	Gen. 25:19-34	Matt. 9:35-10:8	Rom. 5:6-11
Monday	Morning Psalm: 20		Evening Psalm: 126
	Gen. 16:1-14	Matt. 26:1-16	Rom. 6:20-23
Tuesday	Morning Psalm: 41		Evening Psalm: 55
	Gen. 16:15-17:4	Matt. 26:17-25	Rom. 7:1-6
Wednesday	Morning Psalm: 132		Evening Psalm: 128
	Gen. 17:15-27	Matt. 26:26-35	Rom. 7:7-12
Thursday	Morning Psalm: 12		Evening Psalm: 6
	Gen. 18:1-16	Matt. 26:36-46	Rom. 7:13-20
Friday	Morning Psalm: 1		Evening Psalm: 28
	Gen. 18:16-33	Matt. 26:47-56	Rom. 7:21-25
Saturday	Morning Psalm: 107:1-22		Evening Psalm: 107:23-43
	Gen. 19:1-17 (18-23), 24-19	Matt. 26:57-68	Rom. 8:1-8

A Daily Lectionary

Proper 7 (*Sunday between June 19 and 25 if after Trinity Sunday*)

Sunday	Morning Psalm: 108		Evening Psalm: 59
	Gen. 28:10-17	Matt. 10:24-33	Rom. 5:12-19
Monday	Morning Psalm: 38		Evening Psalm: 126
	Gen. 21:1-21	Matt. 26:69-75	Rom. 8:9-17
Tuesday	Morning Psalm: 92		Evening Psalm: 39
	Gen. 22:1-18	Matt. 27:1-10	Rom. 8:18-25
Wednesday	Morning Psalm: 27		Evening Psalm: 139
	Gen. 23:1-20	Matt. 27:11-23	Rom. 8:26-30
Thursday	Morning Psalm: 26		Evening Psalm: 44
	Gen. 24:1-27	Matt. 27:24-31	Rom. 8:31-39
Friday	Morning Psalm: 69:1-18		Evening Psalm: 69:19-36
	Gen. 24:28-38 (39-48), 49-51	Matt. 27:32-44	Acts 13:1-12
Saturday	Morning Psalm: 22:1-21		Evening Psalm: 22:22-31
	Gen. 24:50-67	Matt. 27:45-54	Acts 13:13-25

Proper 8 (*Sunday between June 26 and July 2 inclusive*)

Sunday	Morning Psalm: 29		Evening Psalm: 73
	Gen. 32:22-32	Matt. 10:34-42	Rom. 6:3-11
Monday	Morning Psalm: 2		Evening Psalm: 16
	Gen. 25:19-34	Matt. 27:55-66	Acts 13:26-43
Tuesday	Morning Psalm: 149		Evening Psalm: 124
	Gen. 26:1-6 (7-11), 12-33	Matt. 28:1-10	Acts 13:44-52
Wednesday	Morning Psalm: 101		Evening Psalm: 98
	Gen. 27:1-29	Matt. 28:11-20	Acts 14:1-7
Thursday	Morning Psalm: 146		Evening Psalm: 81
	Gen. 27:30-45	Luke 1:1-25	Acts 14:8-18
Friday	Morning Psalm: 84		Evening Psalm: 85
	Gen. 27:46-28:22	Luke 1:26-38	Acts 14:19-28
Saturday	Morning Psalm: 45		Evening Psalm: 133
	Gen. 29:1-20	Luke 1:29-45a	Acts 15:1-12

Year A

Proper 9 (*Sunday between July 3 and 9 inclusive*)

Sunday	Morning Psalm: 138 Exod. 1:6-14, 22-2:10	Matt. 11:25-30	Evening Psalm: 23 Rom. 7:14-25a
Monday	Morning Psalm: 35 Gen. 29:20-35	Luke 1:48-56	Evening Psalm: 77 Acts 15:12-21
Tuesday	Morning Psalm: 72 Gen. 30:1-24	Luke 1:57-66	Evening Psalm: 145 Acts 15:22-29
Wednesday	Morning Psalm: 18:1-24 Gen. 31:1-24	Luke 1:67-80	Evening Psalm: 18:25-50 Acts 15:30-41
Thursday	Morning Psalm: 37:1-20 Gen. 31:25-50	Luke 2:1-14	Evening Psalm: 37:21-40 Acts 16:1-12
Friday	Morning Psalm: 24 Gen. 32:1-21	Luke 2:15-21	Evening Psalm: 93 Acts 16:13-15
Saturday	Morning Psalm: 43 Gen. 32:22-33:17	Luke 2:22-32	Evening Psalm: 97 Acts 16:16-24

Proper 10 (*Sunday between July 10 and 16 inclusive*)

Sunday	Morning Psalm: 65 Exod. 2:11-22	Matt. 13:1-9, 18-23	Evening Psalm: 33 Rom. 8:9-17
Monday	Morning Psalm: 76 Gen. 35:1-20	Luke 2:33-40	Evening Psalm: 47 Acts 16:25-34
Tuesday	Morning Psalm: 122 Gen. 37:1-11	Luke 2:41-52	Evening Psalm: 15 Acts 16:35-40
Wednesday	Morning Psalm: 25 Gen. 37:12-24	Luke 3:1-14	Evening Psalm: 143 Acts 17:1-4
Thursday	Morning Psalm: 56 Gen. 37:25-36	Luke 3:15-22	Evening Psalm: 7 Acts 17:5-10
Friday	Morning Psalm: 120 Gen. 39:1-23	Luke 4:1-13	Evening Psalm: 91 Acts 17:11-15
Saturday	Morning Psalm: 123 Gen. 40:1-23	Luke 4:14-21	Evening Psalm: 70 Acts 17:16-20

A Daily Lectionary

Proper 11 (*Sunday between July 17 and 23 inclusive*)

Sunday	Morning Psalm: 86		Evening Psalm: 117
	Exod. 3:1-12	Matt. 13:24-30, 36-43	Rom. 8:18-25
Monday	Morning Psalm: 57		Evening Psalm: 113
	Gen. 41:1-13	Luke 4:22-30	Acts 17:21-28
Tuesday	Morning Psalm: 50		Evening Psalm: 94
	Gen. 41:14-45	Luke 4:31-37	Acts 17:29-34
Wednesday	Morning Psalm: 88		Evening Psalm: 30
	Gen. 41:46-57	Luke 4:38-44	Acts 18:1-11
Thursday	Morning Psalm: 79		Evening Psalm: 13
	Gen. 42:1-17	Luke 5:1-11	Acts 18:12-21
Friday	Morning Psalm: 42		Evening Psalm: 141
	Gen. 42:18-28	Luke 5:12-26	Acts 18:22-28
Saturday	Morning Psalm: 63		Evening Psalm: 111
	Gen. 42:29-38	Luke 5:27-39	Acts 19:1-7

Proper 12 (*Sunday between July 24 and 30 inclusive*)

Sunday	Morning Psalm: 135		Evening Psalm: 95
	Exod. 3:13-20	Matt. 13:44-52	Rom. 8:26-30
Monday	Morning Psalm: 21		Evening Psalm: 133
	Gen. 43:1-15	Luke 6:1-11	Acts 19:8-10
Tuesday	Morning Psalm: 67		Evening Psalm: 4
	Gen. 43:16-34	Luke 6:12-26	Acts 19:11-20
Wednesday	Morning Psalm: 96		Evening Psalm: 90
	Gen. 44:1-17	Luke 6:27-38	Acts 19:21-28
Thursday	Morning Psalm: 71		Evening Psalm: 36
	Gen. 44:18-34	Luke 6:39-49	Acts 19:29-41
Friday	Morning Psalm: 17		Evening Psalm: 20
	Gen. 45:1-15	Luke 7:1-17	Acts 20:1-6
Saturday	Morning Psalm: 18:1-30		Evening Psalm: 18:31-50
	Gen. 45:16-28	Luke 7:18-35	Acts 20:7-12

Year A

Proper 13 (*Sunday between July 31 and August 6 inclusive*)

Sunday	Morning Psalm: 136		Evening Psalm: 134
	Exod. 12:1-14	Matt. 14:13-21	Rom. 8:31-39
Monday	Morning Psalm: 59		Evening Psalm: 9
	Gen. 46:1-7, 28-34	Luke 7:36-50	Acts 20:13-27
Tuesday	Morning Psalm: 102		Evening Psalm: 125
	Gen. 47:1-26	Luke 8:1-15	Acts 20:28-35
Wednesday	Morning Psalm: 61		Evening Psalm: 114
	Gen. 47:27-48:7	Luke 8:16-25	Acts 21:1-6
Thursday	Morning Psalm: 140		Evening Psalm: 46
	Gen. 48:8-22	Luke 8:26-39	Acts 21:7-16
Friday	Morning Psalm: 142		Evening Psalm: 60
	Gen. 49:1-28	Luke 8:40-56	Acts 21:17-26
Saturday	Morning Psalm: 83		Evening Psalm: 129
	Gen. 49:29-50:14	Luke 9:1-17	Acts 21:27-36

Proper 14 (*Sunday between August 7 and 13 inclusive*)

Sunday	Morning Psalm: 137		Evening Psalm: 85
	Exod. 14:19-31	Matt. 14:22-33	Rom. 9:1-5
Monday	Morning Psalm: 54		Evening Psalm: 68
	Gen. 50:15-26	Luke 9:18-27	Rom. 9:6-13
Tuesday	Morning Psalm: 3		Evening Psalm: 74
	Exod. 1:6-22	Luke 9:28-36	Rom. 9:14-18
Wednesday	Morning Psalm: 11		Evening Psalm: 4
	Exod. 2:1-22	Luke 9:37-50	Rom. 9:19-27
Thursday	Morning Psalm: 52		Evening Psalm: 82
	Exod. 2:23-3:15	Luke 9:51-62	Rom. 9:28-33
Friday	Morning Psalm: 75		Evening Psalm: 64
	Exod. 3:16-4:12	Luke 10:1-16	Rom. 10:1-4
Saturday	Morning Psalm: 58		Evening Psalm: 48
	Exod. 4:10-20 (21-26), 27-31	Luke 10:17-24	Rom. 10:5-9

A Daily Lectionary

Proper 15 (*Sunday between August 14 and 20 inclusive*)

Sunday	Morning Psalm: 78:1-31		Evening Psalm: 78:32-72
	Exod. 16:2-15	Matt. 15:21-28	Rom. 11:13-16, 29-32
Monday	Morning Psalm: 109		Evening Psalm: 44
	Exod. 5:1-6:1	Luke 10:25-37	Rom. 10:10-13
Tuesday	Morning Psalm: 131		Evening Psalm: 28
	Exod. 7:8-24	Luke 10:38-42	Rom. 10:14-16
Wednesday	Morning Psalm: 65		Evening Psalm: 73
	Exod. 7:25-8:19	Luke 11:1-13	Rom. 10:17-20
Thursday	Morning Psalm: 12		Evening Psalm: 1
	Exod. 3:19-35	Luke 11:14-26	Rom. 10:21-11:6
Friday	Morning Psalm: 105:1-22		Evening Psalm: 105:23-45
	Exod. 10:21-11:8	Luke 11:27-36	Rom. 11:7-12
Saturday	Morning Psalm: 146		Evening Psalm: 136
	Exod. 12:14-27	Luke 11:37-52	Rom. 11:13-21

Proper 16 (*Sunday between August 21 and 27 inclusive*)

Sunday	Morning Psalm: 117		Evening Psalm: 138
	Exod. 17:1-7	Matt. 16:13-20	Rom. 11:33-36
Monday	Morning Psalm: 120		Evening Psalm: 135
	Exod. 12:14-27	Luke 11:53-12:12	Rom. 11:22-24
Tuesday	Morning Psalm: 99		Evening Psalm: 39
	Exod. 12:28-39	Luke 12:13-31	Rom. 11:25-28
Wednesday	Morning Psalm: 116		Evening Psalm: 112
	Exod. 12:40-51	Luke 12:32-48	Rom. 11:29-36
Thursday	Morning Psalm: 1		Evening Psalm: 115
	Exod. 13:3-10	Luke 12:49-59	Rom. 12:1-2
Friday	Morning Psalm: 97		Evening Psalm: 37
	Exod. 13:1-2, 11-16	Luke 13:1-9	Rom. 12:3-8
Saturday	Morning Psalm: 103		Evening Psalm: 6
	Exod. 13:17-14:4	Luke 13:10-17	Rom. 12:9-13

Year A

Proper 17 (*Sunday between August 28 and September 3 inclusive*)
Sunday	Morning Psalm: 26		Evening Psalm: 9
	Exod. 19:1-9	Matt. 16:21-28	Rom. 12:1-13
Monday	Morning Psalm: 106:1-23		Evening Psalm: 106:24-48
	Exod. 14:5-22	Luke 13:18-30	Rom. 12:14-21
Tuesday	Morning Psalm: 18:1-24		Evening Psalm: 18:25-50
	Exod. 14:21-31	Luke 13:31-35	Rom. 13:1-7
Wednesday	Morning Psalm: 50		Evening Psalm: 77
	Exod. 15:1-21	Luke 14:1-11	Rom. 13:8-10
Thursday	Morning Psalm: 36		Evening Psalm: 95
	Exod. 15:22-16:10	Luke 14:12-24	Rom. 13:11-14
Friday	Morning Psalm: 63		Evening Psalm: 111
	Exod. 16:10-22	Luke 14:25-35	Rom. 14:1-4
Saturday	Morning Psalm: 145		Evening Psalm: 23
	Exod. 16:23-36	Luke 15:1-10	Rom. 14:5-9

Proper 18 (*Sunday between September 4 and 10 inclusive*)
Sunday	Morning Psalm: 119:1-24		Evening Psalm: 119:25-48
	Exod. 19:16-24	Matt. 18:15-20	Rom. 13:1-10
Monday	Morning Psalm: 114		Evening Psalm: 81
	Exod. 17:1-16	Luke 15:11-32	Rom. 14:10-13
Tuesday	Morning Psalm: 133		Evening Psalm: 68
	Exod. 18:1-12	Luke 16:1-9	Rom. 14:14-18
Wednesday	Morning Psalm: 34		Evening Psalm: 119:49-72
	Exod. 18:13-27	Luke 16:10-18	Rom. 14:19-23
Thursday	Morning Psalm: 41		Evening Psalm: 119:73-96
	Exod. 19:1-16	Luke 16:19-31	Rom. 15:1-6
Friday	Morning Psalm: 119:97-120		Evening Psalm: 119:121-152
	Exod. 19:16-25	Luke 17:1-10	Rom. 15:7-13
Saturday	Morning Psalm: 19		Evening Psalm: 119:153-176
	Exod. 20:1-20	Luke 17:11-19	Rom. 15:14-17

A Daily Lectionary

Proper 19 (*Sunday between September 11 and 17 inclusive*)

Sunday	Morning Psalm: 25 Exod. 20:1-20	Matt. 18:21-35	Evening Psalm: 86 Rom. 14:5-12
Monday	Morning Psalm: 96 Exod. 24:1-18	Luke 17:20-37	Evening Psalm: 93 Rom. 15:18-21
Tuesday	Morning Psalm: 3 Exod. 25:1-22	Luke 18:1-8	Evening Psalm: 80 Rom. 15:22-33
Wednesday	Morning Psalm: 5 Exod. 28:1-4, 30-38	Luke 18:9-14	Evening Psalm: 110 Rom. 16:1-16
Thursday	Morning Psalm: 38 Exod. 32:1-20	Luke 18:15-30	Evening Psalm: 53 Rom. 16:17-27
Friday	Morning Psalm: 69:1-18 Exod. 32:21-34	Luke 18:31-43	Evening Psalm: 69:19-36 Phil. 1:1-11
Saturday	Morning Psalm: 32 Exod. 33:1-23	Luke 19:1-10	Evening Psalm: 84 Phil. 1:12-20

Proper 20 (*Sunday between September 18 and 24 inclusive*)

Sunday	Morning Psalm: 150 Exod. 32:1-14	Matt. 20:1-16	Evening Psalm: 27 Phil. 1:21-27
Monday	Morning Psalm: 16 Exod. 34:1-17	Luke 19:11-27	Evening Psalm: 85 Phil. 1:27-30
Tuesday	Morning Psalm: 24 Exod. 34:18-35	Luke 19:28-40	Evening Psalm: 118 Phil. 2:1-5
Wednesday	Morning Psalm: 87 Exod. 40:18-38	Luke 19:41-48	Evening Psalm: 48 Phil. 2:6-13
Thursday	Morning Psalm: 133 Lev. 8:1-13, 30-36	Luke 20:1-8	Evening Psalm: 110 Phil. 2:14-18
Friday	Morning Psalm: 51 Lev. 16:1-19	Luke 20:9-18	Evening Psalm: 79 Phil. 2:19-30
Saturday	Morning Psalm: 50 Lev. 16:20-34	Luke 20:19-26	Evening Psalm: 31 Phil. 3:1-7

Year A

Proper 21 (*Sunday between September 25 and October 1 inclusive*)

Sunday	Morning Psalm: 40		Evening Psalm: 134
	Exod. 33:12-23	Matt. 21:28-32	Phil. 2:1-13
Monday	Morning Psalm: 15		Evening Psalm: 42
	Lev. 19:1-18	Luke 20:27-40	Phil. 3:8-11
Tuesday	Morning Psalm: 54		Evening Psalm: 113
	Lev. 19:26-37	Luke 20:41-21:4	Phil. 3:12-21
Wednesday	Morning Psalm: 75		Evening Psalm: 82
	Lev. 23:1-22	Luke 21:5-19	Phil. 4:1-7
Thursday	Morning Psalm: 2		Evening Psalm: 58
	Lev. 23:23-34	Luke 21:20-28	Phil. 4:8-13
Friday	Morning Psalm: 29		Evening Psalm: 46
	Lev. 25:1-17	Luke 21:29-38	Phil. 4:14-23
Saturday	Morning Psalm: 55		Evening Psalm: 49
	Lev. 25:35-55	Luke 22:1-13	Eph. 1:1-10

Proper 22 (*Sunday between October 2 and 8 inclusive*)

Sunday	Morning Psalm: 148		Evening Psalm: 80
	Num. 27:12-23	Matt. 21:33-43	Phil. 3:12-21
Monday	Morning Psalm: 67		Evening Psalm: 141
	Lev. 26:1-20	Luke 22:14-30	Eph. 1:11-15
Tuesday	Morning Psalm: 70		Evening Psalm: 60
	Lev. 26:27-42	Luke 22:31-38	Eph. 1:16-23
Wednesday	Morning Psalm: 130		Evening Psalm: 7
	Num. 3:1-13	Luke 22:39-53	Eph. 2:1-10
Thursday	Morning Psalm: 62		Evening Psalm: 4
	Num. 6:22-27	Luke 22:54-71	Eph. 2:11-23
Friday	Morning Psalm: 57		Evening Psalm: 73
	Num. 9:15-23	Luke 23:1-12	Eph. 3:1-6
Saturday	Morning Psalm: 52		Evening Psalm: 43
	Num. 10:29-36	Luke 23:13-25	Eph. 3:7-13

A Daily Lectionary

Proper 23 (*Sunday between October 9 and 15 inclusive*)

Sunday	Morning Psalm: 45		Evening Psalm: 22:1-21
	Deut. 34:1-12	Matt. 22:1-14	Phil. 4:1-9
Monday	Morning Psalm: 144		Evening Psalm: 22:22-31
	Num. 11:1-23	Luke 23:26-31	Eph. 3:14-21
Tuesday	Morning Psalm: 69:1-18		Evening Psalm: 69:19-36
	Num. 11:24-35	Luke 23:32-43	Eph. 4:1-6
Wednesday	Morning Psalm: 56		Evening Psalm: 10
	Num. 12:1-16	Luke 23:44-56a	Eph. 4:7-16
Thursday	Morning Psalm: 30		Evening Psalm: 33
	Num. 13:1-3, 21-30	Luke 23:56b-24:11	Eph. 4:17-24
Friday	Morning Psalm: 61		Evening Psalm: 20
	Num. 13:31-14:25	Luke 24:12-35	Eph. 4:25-32
Saturday	Morning Psalm: 66		Evening Psalm: 91
	Num. 14:26-45	Luke 24:36-53	Eph. 5:1-14

Proper 24 (*Sunday between October 16 and 22 inclusive*)

Sunday	Morning Psalm: 149		Evening Psalm: 90
	Ruth 1:1-19a (19b-22)	Matt. 22:15-22	1 Thess. 1:1-10
Monday	Morning Psalm: 143		Evening Psalm: 124
	Num. 16:1-19	Matt. 5:1-10	Eph. 5:1-15
Tuesday	Morning Psalm: 71		Evening Psalm: 126
	Num. 16:20-35	Matt. 5:11-16	Eph. 5:25-33
Wednesday	Morning Psalm: 14		Evening Psalm: 35
	Num. 16:36-50	Matt. 5:17-20	Eph. 6:1-9
Thursday	Morning Psalm: 83		Evening Psalm: 92
	Num. 17:1-11	Matt. 5:21-26	Eph. 6:10-17
Friday	Morning Psalm: 104		Evening Psalm: 127
	Num. 20:1-13	Matt. 5:27-37	Eph. 6:18-24
Saturday	Morning Psalm: 17		Evening Psalm: 107
	Num. 20:14-29	Matt. 5:38-48	2 Thess. 1:1-5

Year A

Proper 25 (*Sunday between October 23 and 29 inclusive*)

Sunday	Morning Psalm: 100		Evening Psalm: 11
	Ruth 2:1-13	Matt. 22:34-46	1 Thess. 2:1-8
Monday	Morning Psalm: 107:1-22		Evening Psalm: 107:23-43
	Num. 21:4-9, 21-35	Matt. 6:1-6, 16-18	2 Thess. 1:6-12
Tuesday	Morning Psalm: 108		Evening Psalm: 8
	Num. 22:1-21	Matt. 6:7-15	2 Thess. 2:1-4
Wednesday	Morning Psalm: 140		Evening Psalm: 64
	Num. 22:21-38	Matt. 6:19-24	2 Thess. 2:5-12
Thursday	Morning Psalm: 142		Evening Psalm: 128
	Num. 22:41-23:12	Matt. 6:25-34	2 Thess. 2:13-17
Friday	Morning Psalm: 122		Evening Psalm: 129
	Num. 23:11-26	Matt. 7:1-12	2 Thess. 3:1-6
Saturday	Morning Psalm: 137		Evening Psalm: 102
	Num. 24:1-13	Matt. 7:13-21	2 Thess. 3:7-18

Proper 26 (*Sunday between October 30 and November 5 inclusive*)

Sunday	Morning Psalm: 88		Evening Psalm: 11
	Ruth 4:7-17 (18-22)	Matt. 23:1-12	1 Thess. 2:9-13, 17-20
Monday	Morning Psalm: 150		Evening Psalm: 13
	Num. 24:12-25	Matt. 23:13-22	1 Thess. 2:14-16
Tuesday	Morning Psalm: 15		Evening Psalm: 19
	Num. 27:12-23	Matt. 23:23-28	1 Thess. 3:1-5
Wednesday	Morning Psalm: 118		Evening Psalm: 74
	Num. 32:1-6, 16-27	Matt. 23:29-39	1 Thess. 3:6-10
Thursday	Morning Psalm: 37		Evening Psalm: 14
	Num. 35:1-3, 9-15, 30-34	Matt. 24:1-14	1 Thess. 3:11-13
Friday	Morning Psalm: 97		Evening Psalm: 94
	Ruth 2:1-13	Matt. 24:15-28	1 Thess. 4:1-8
Saturday	Morning Psalm: 119:73-96		Evening Psalm: 8
	Ruth 2:14-23	Matt. 24:29-35	1 Thess. 4:9-12

A Daily Lectionary

Proper 27 (*Sunday between November 6 and 12 inclusive*)

Sunday	Morning Psalm: 63 Amos 5:18-24	Matt. 25:1-13	Evening Psalm: 117 1 Thess. 4:13-18
Monday	Morning Psalm: 76 Ruth 3:1-13	Matt. 24:36-43	Evening Psalm: 90 2 Pet. 1:1-4
Tuesday	Morning Psalm: 1 Ruth 3:14-4:6	Matt. 24:44-51	Evening Psalm: 81 2 Pet. 1:5-11
Wednesday	Morning Psalm: 25 Amos 1:1-15	John 11:1-16	Evening Psalm: 33 2 Pet. 1:12-21
Thursday	Morning Psalm: 83 Amos 2:1-16	John 11:17-29	Evening Psalm: 116 2 Pet. 2:1-10a
Friday	Morning Psalm: 124 Amos 3:1-15	John 11:30-44	Evening Psalm: 74 2 Pet. 2:10b-16
Saturday	Morning Psalm: 140 Amos 4:1-13	John 11:45-54	Evening Psalm: 139 2 Pet. 2:17-22

Proper 28 (*Sunday between November 13 and 19 inclusive*)

Sunday	Morning Psalm: 93 Zeph. 1:7, 12-18	Matt. 25:14-30	Evening Psalm: 128 1 Thess. 5:1-11
Monday	Morning Psalm: 97 Amos 5:1-25	John 11:55-12:8	Evening Psalm: 74 1 Thess. 5:12-28
Tuesday	Morning Psalm: 75 Amos 6:1-14	John 12:9-19	Evening Psalm: 118 2 Pet. 3:1-7
Wednesday	Morning Psalm: 37:1-22 Amos 7:1-17	John 12:20-26	Evening Psalm: 37:23-40 2 Pet. 3:8-13
Thursday	Morning Psalm: 58 Amos 8:1-14	Luke 19:11-27	Evening Psalm: 14 2 Pet. 3:14-18
Friday	Morning Psalm: 80 Amos 9:1-15	Luke 19:28-40	Evening Psalm: 139 1 Cor. 15:1-11
Saturday	Morning Psalm: 87 Isa. 19:19-25	Luke 19:41-48	Evening Psalm: 48 1 Cor. 15:12-20

Year A

Christ the King Sunday

Sunday	Morning Psalm: 72		Evening Psalm: 47
	Ezek. 34:11-16, 20-24	Matt. 25:31-46	1 Cor. 15:20-28
Monday	Morning Psalm: 87		Evening Psalm: 139
	Joel 3:1-2, 9-17	Matt. 22:41-46	Eph. 1:16-23
Tuesday	Morning Psalm: 89:1-18		Evening Psalm: 89:19-51
	Nah. 1:1-13	Mark 13:1-8	Eph. 3:8-19
Wednesday	Morning Psalm: 147		Evening Psalm: 94
	Obad. 15-21	Mark 13:9-16	Phil. 3:17-21
Thursday	Morning Psalm: 76		Evening Psalm: 121
	Zeph. 3:1-13	Mark 13:17-23	2 Thess. 2:1-6
Friday	Morning Psalm: 98		Evening Psalm: 125
	Isa. 24:14-23	Mark 13:24-31	2 Thess. 2:7-12
Saturday	Morning Psalm: 123		Evening Psalm: 132
	Mic. 7:11-20	Luke 21:5-19	Rom. 8:18-25

6
YEAR B

Advent 1

Sunday	Morning Psalm: 80 Isa. 63:16-64:8	Mark 13:21-37	Evening Psalm: 97 1 Cor. 1:3-9
Monday	Morning Psalm: 12 Hos. 4:1-10	Luke 21:20-28	Evening Psalm: 53 2 Pet. 1:1-11
Tuesday	Morning Psalm: 2 Hos. 4:11-16	Luke 21:29-36	Evening Psalm: 14 2 Pet. 1:12-21
Wednesday	Morning Psalm: 93 Hos. 5:1-14	Matt. 3:1-10	Evening Psalm: 39 2 Pet. 3:1-10
Thursday	Morning Psalm: 39 Hos 5:15-6:10	Matt. 3:11-17	Evening Psalm: 19 2 Pet. 3:11-18
Friday	Morning Psalm: 146 Hos. 6:11-7:7	Matt. 11:2-10	Evening Psalm: 145 Rev. 2:2-7
Saturday	Morning Psalm: 60 Hos. 8:1-10	Matt. 11:11-19	Evening Psalm: 79 Acts 17:24-31

Advent 2

Sunday	Morning Psalm: 72 Isa. 40:1-11	Mark 1:1-8	Evening Psalm: 117 2 Pet. 3:8-15a
Monday	Morning Psalm: 40 Hos. 8:11-14	Matt. 20:20-28	Evening Psalm: 32 1 Pet. 1:13-25
Tuesday	Morning Psalm: 80 Hos. 10:1-12	Matt. 17:9-13	Evening Psalm: 36 Acts 19:1-7
Wednesday	Morning Psalm: 78:1-39 Hos. 11:1-7	Matt. 23:1-12	Evening Psalm: 78:40-72 Acts 13:16-25
Thursday	Morning Psalm: 100 Hos. 11:8-12	Matt. 23:13-22	Evening Psalm: 86 Phil. 4:4-7
Friday	Morning Psalm: 50 Hos. 12:2-9	Matt. 23:23-28	Evening Psalm: 49 1 Thess. 5:1-7
Saturday	Morning Psalm: 52 Hos. 13:4-9	Matt. 23:29-39	Evening Psalm: 10 1 Thess. 5:8-15

Year B

Advent 3

Sunday	Morning Psalm: 146 Isa. 61:1-4, 8-11	John 1:6-8, 19-28	Evening Psalm: 45 1 Thess. 5:16-24
Monday	Morning Psalm: 37 Hos. 14:1-9	Matt. 23:1-14	Evening Psalm: 91 Jude 1-16
Tuesday	Morning Psalm: 99 Mal. 3:1-5	Matt. 24:15-31	Evening Psalm: 112 Jude 17-25
Wednesday	Morning Psalm: 103 Mal. 3:6-12	Matt. 24:32-44	Evening Psalm: 46 James 5:7-10
Thursday	Morning Psalm: 56 Mal. 3:13-18	Matt. 24:45-51	Evening Psalm: 73 Rom. 11:33-36
Friday	Morning Psalm: 43 Mal. 4:1-5	Matt. 25:1-13	Evening Psalm: 44 1 Cor. 2:1-6
Saturday	Morning Psalm: 27 Exod. 15:11-18	Matt. 25:14-30	Evening Psalm: 74 1 Cor. 2:7-13

Advent 4*

Sunday	Morning Psalm: 24 2 Sam. 7:8-16	Luke 1:26-38	Evening Psalm: 134 Rom. 16:25-27
Monday	Morning Psalm: 75 1 Chron. 16:8-18	Matt. 25:31-46	Evening Psalm: 77 Eph. 3:7-13
Tuesday	Morning Psalm: 96 1 Chron. 16:19-27	John 5:30-47	Evening Psalm: 48 Col. 1:24-29
Wednesday	Morning Psalm: 98 1 Chron. 16:28-36	John 6:27-34	Evening Psalm: 29 Rev. 21:1-8
Thursday	Morning Psalm: 89:1-25 1 Chron. 17:1-10	John 6:35-51	Evening Psalm: 89:26-52 Rev. 21:9-21
Friday	Morning Psalm: 144 2 Sam. 7:18-22	John 1:9-18	Evening Psalm: 132 Rev. 21:22-22:5
Saturday	Morning Psalm: 18:1-24 2 Sam. 7:23-29	John 3:16-21	Evening Psalm: 18:25-50 Rev. 22:12-17, 21

Christmas Eve

	Morning Psalm: 85 Isa. 9:2-7	Luke 2:1-20	Evening Psalm: 110 Titus 2:11-14

Skip to Christmas Eve lesson on Christmas Eve.

A Daily Lectionary

Christmas Day

	Morning Psalm: 2		Evening Psalm: 34
	Isa. 62:6-7, 10-12, or	Luke 2:8-20 or	Titus 3:4-7 or
	Isa. 52:7-10	John 1:1-14	Heb. 1:1-12
Dec. 26	Morning Psalm: 150		Evening Psalm: 126
	2 Chron. 24:17-22	Acts 7:55-8:8	Acts 6:1-7
Dec. 27	Morning Psalm: 99		Evening Psalm: 97
	Prov. 8:22-30	John 13:2-20	1 John 5:1-12
Dec. 28	Morning Psalm: 116		Evening Psalm: 7
	Isa. 49:13-23	Matt. 18:1-14	1 John 4:7-16
Dec. 29	Morning Psalm: 147		Evening Psalm: 65
	Isa. 12:1-6	John 7:37-52	Rev. 1:1-8
Dec. 30	Morning Psalm: 118		Evening Psalm: 51
	Isa. 25:1-9	John 7:53-8:11	Rev. 1:9-20
Dec. 31	Morning Psalm: 28		Evening Psalm: 90
	Isa. 26:1-6	John 8:12-19	2 Cor. 5:16-6:2

1st Sunday after Christmas*

	Morning Psalm: 149		Evening Psalm: 111
	Isa. 61:10-62:3	Luke 2:22-40 or	Gal. 4:4-7
		John 1:1-18	
Jan. 1	Morning Psalm: 21		Evening Psalm: 92
	Eccles. 3:1-13	Matt. 9:14-17	Col. 2:1-7
Jan. 2	Morning Psalm: 105:1-25		Evening Psalm: 105:26-45
	Gen. 12:1-7	John 6:35-42, 48-51	Heb. 11:1-12
Jan. 3	Morning Psalm: 25		Evening Psalm: 23
	Gen. 28:10-22	John 10:7-17	Heb. 11:13-22
Jan. 4	Morning Psalm: 106:1-23		Evening Psalm: 106:24-48
	Exod. 3:1-15	John 14:6-14	Heb. 11:23-31
Jan. 5	Morning Psalm: 133		Evening Psalm: 82
	Josh. 1:1-9	John 15:1-16	Heb. 11:32-12:2

2nd Sunday after Christmas**

	Morning Psalm: 107:1-22	Evening Psalm: 107:23-43
	Jer. 31:7-14	John 1:1-18	Eph. 1:3-6, 12-20

*When a Sunday lesson coincides with a dated lesson, the Sunday lesson should be read.

**If this is Epiphany, skip to Epiphany reading. This lesson is not read during years in which only one Sunday falls between Christmas and Epiphany.

Year B

Epiphany	Morning Psalm: 72		Evening Psalm: 68
	Isa. 60:1-6	Matt. 2:1-12	Eph. 3:1-12
Jan. 7	Morning Psalm: 45		Evening Psalm: 44
	Isa. 52:3-6	John 2:1-11	Rev. 2:1-7
Jan. 8	Morning Psalm: 5		Evening Psalm: 113
	Isa. 59:15b-21	John 4:46-54	Rev. 2:8-17
Jan. 9	Morning Psalm: 83		Evening Psalm: 62
	Isa. 63:1-5	John 5:1-15	Rev. 2:18-29
Jan. 10	Morning Psalm: 93		Evening Psalm: 11
	Isa. 65:1-9	John 6:1-14	Rev. 3:1-6
Jan. 11	Morning Psalm: 101		Evening Psalm: 81
	Isa. 65:13-16	John 6:15-27	Rev. 3:7-13
Jan. 12	Morning Psalm: 15		Evening Psalm: 16
	Isa. 66:1-2, 22-23	John 9:1-12, 35-38	Rev. 3:14-22

1st Sunday after Epiphany*

Sunday	Morning Psalm: 148		Evening Psalm: 29
	Gen. 1:1-5	Mark 4:1-11	Acts 19:1-7
Monday	Morning Psalm: 104:1-13	Evening Psalm: 104:14-35	
	Isa. 40:21-31	Mark 4:13-20	Rev. 3:14-22
Tuesday	Morning Psalm: 18:1-24	Evening Psalm: 18:25-50	
	Isa. 45:1-8	Mark 4:21-31	Heb. 1:1-11
Wednesday	Morning Psalm: 119:25-48	Evening Psalm: 119:49-72	
	Isa. 45:9-17	Matt. 4:12-17	1 Cor. 1:1-9
Thursday	Morning Psalm: 119:73-96	Evening Psalm: 119:97-120	
	Isa. 45:18-25	Matt. 4:18-25	1 Cor. 1:10-17
Friday	Morning Psalm: 71		Evening Psalm: 129
	Isa. 46:1-13	John 1:1-18	1 Cor. 1:18-25
Saturday	Morning Psalm: 123		Evening Psalm: 115
	Isa. 47:1-15	John 1:19-34	1 Cor. 1:26-31

*Begin this week of readings on the first Sunday after Epiphany, skipping any dated material necessary.

A Daily Lectionary

2nd Sunday after Epiphany

Sunday	Morning Psalm: 67 1 Sam. 3:1-10 (11-20)	John 1:35-42	Evening Psalm: 119:121-152 1 Cor. 6:12-20
Monday	Morning Psalm: 58 Isa. 48:1-11	John 1:43-51	Evening Psalm: 8 1 Cor. 2:1-9
Tuesday	Morning Psalm: 102 Isa. 48:12-22	John 2:1-12	Evening Psalm: 119:153-176 1 Cor. 2:10-16
Wednesday	Morning Psalm: 22:1-15 Isa. 49:1-7	John 2:13-22	Evening Psalm: 22:16-31 1 Cor. 3:1-9
Thursday	Morning Psalm: 109 Jon. 1:1-16	John 2:23-3:15	Evening Psalm: 139 1 Cor. 3:10-17
Friday	Morning Psalm: 88 Jon. 1:17-2:10	John 3:16-21	Evening Psalm: 130 1 Cor. 3:18-23
Saturday	Morning Psalm: 54 Jon. 3:1-10	John 3:22-36	Evening Psalm: 9 1 Cor. 4:1-5

3rd Sunday after Epiphany

Sunday	Morning Psalm: 133 Jon. 3:1-5, 10	Mark 1:14-20	Evening Psalm: 94 1 Cor. 7:29-31 (32-35)
Monday	Morning Psalm: 136 Jon. 3:10-4:11	John 4:1-15	Evening Psalm: 124 1 Cor. 4:6-13
Tuesday	Morning Psalm: 1 Josh. 1:1-9	John 4:16-26	Evening Psalm: 84 1 Cor. 4:14-21
Wednesday	Morning Psalm: 26 Josh. 1:10-18	John 4:27-42	Evening Psalm: 141 1 Cor. 5:1-5
Thursday	Morning Psalm: 38 Josh. 2:1-14	John 4:43-54	Evening Psalm: 64 1 Cor. 5:6-13
Friday	Morning Psalm: 76 Josh. 2:15-24	John 5:1-18	Evening Psalm: 17 1 Cor. 6:1-8
Saturday	Morning Psalm: 108 Josh. 3:1-10	John 5:19-29	Evening Psalm: 20 1 Cor. 6:9-11

Year B

4th Sunday after Epiphany*

Sunday	Morning Psalm: 57 Deut. 18:15-20	Mark 1:21-28	Evening Psalm: 1 1 Cor. 8:1-13
Monday	Morning Psalm: 70 Josh. 3:9-17	John 5:30-47	Evening Psalm: 66 1 Cor. 6:12-20
Tuesday	Morning Psalm: 63 Josh. 4:1-18	John 6:1-15	Evening Psalm: 47 1 Cor. 7:1-7
Wednesday	Morning Psalm: 131 Josh. 4:19-5:1	John 6:16-27	Evening Psalm: 121 1 Cor. 7:8-11
Thursday	Morning Psalm: 61 Josh. 5:2-15	John 6:28-40	Evening Psalm: 59 1 Cor. 7:12-16
Friday	Morning Psalm: 42 Josh. 6:1-14	John 6:41-51	Evening Psalm: 135 1 Cor. 7:17-24
Saturday	Morning Psalm: 143 Josh. 6:15-27	John 6:52-59	Evening Psalm: 33 1 Cor. 7:25-31

5th Sunday after Epiphany*

Sunday	Morning Psalm: 147 Job 7:1-7	Mark 1:29-39	Evening Psalm: 6 1 Cor. 9:16-23
Monday	Morning Psalm: 106 Josh. 7:1-15	John 6:60-71	Evening Psalm: 55 1 Cor. 7:32-40
Tuesday	Morning Psalm: 120 Josh. 7:16-26	John 7:1-13	Evening Psalm: 4 1 Cor. 8:1-6
Wednesday	Morning Psalm: 95 Josh. 8:1-21	John 7:14-24	Evening Psalm: 31 1 Cor. 8:7-13
Thursday	Morning Psalm: 69:1-15 Josh. 8:30-35	John 7:25-36	Evening Psalm: 69:16-36 1 Cor. 9:1-12a
Friday	Morning Psalm: 3 Josh. 9:3-16, 22-27	John 7:37-52	Evening Psalm: 18:1-24 1 Cor. 9:12b-18
Saturday	Morning Psalm: 140 Josh. 10:1-15	John 7:53-8:11	Evening Psalm: 18:25-50 1 Cor. 9:19-27

If this is last Sunday after Epiphany, skip to Transfiguration Sunday.

A Daily Lectionary

Proper 1 (*6th Sunday after Epiphany*)*

Sunday	Morning Psalm: 32		Evening Psalm: 134
	2 Kings 5:1-14	Mark 1:40-45	1 Cor. 9:24-27
Monday	Morning Psalm: 105:1-22		Evening Psalm: 115
	Josh. 23:1-16	John 8:12-20	1 Cor. 10:1-13
Tuesday	Morning Psalm: 13		Evening Psalm: 105:23-45
	Josh. 24:1-15	John 8:21-30	1 Cor. 10:14-22
Wednesday	Morning Psalm: 87		Evening Psalm: 35
	Josh. 24:16-23	John 8:31-41a	1 Cor. 10:23-11:1
Thursday	Morning Psalm: 41		Evening Psalm: 142
	Esther 1:1-19	John 8:41b-47	2 Cor. 1:1-7
Friday	Morning Psalm: 137		Evening Psalm: 127
	Esther 2:5-8, 15-23	John 8:47-59	2 Cor. 1:8-11
Saturday	Morning Psalm: 122		Evening Psalm: 125
	Esther 3:1-4:3	John 9:1-7	2 Cor. 1:12-20

Proper 2 (*7th Sunday after Epiphany*)*

Sunday	Morning Psalm: 41		Evening Psalm: 128
	1 Sam. 43:18-25	Mark 2:1-12	2 Cor. 1:18-22
Monday	Morning Psalm: 117		Evening Psalm: 31
	Esther 4:4-17	John 9:8-17	2 Cor. 1:23-2:4
Tuesday	Morning Psalm: 55		Evening Psalm: 138
	Esther 5:1-14	John 9:18-41	2 Cor. 2:5-11
Wednesday	Morning Psalm: 40		Evening Psalm: 27
	Esther 6:1-14	John 10:1-6	2 Cor. 2:12-17
Thursday	Morning Psalm: 7		Evening Psalm: 23
	Esther 7:1-10	John 10:7-18	2 Cor. 3:1-3
Friday	Morning Psalm: 92		Evening Psalm: 46
	Esther 8:1-8, 15-17; 9:20-22	John 10:19-30	2 Cor. 3:4-6
Saturday	Morning Psalm: 122		Evening Psalm: 87
	Ezra 1:1-11	John 10:31-42	2 Cor. 3:7-11

If this is last Sunday after Epiphany, skip to Transfiguration Sunday.

Year B

Proper 3 (*8th Sunday after Epiphany*)*

Sunday	Morning Psalm: 103 Hos. 2:14-20	Mark 2:18-22	Evening Psalm: 145 2 Cor. 3:1-6
Monday	Morning Psalm: 84 Ezra 3:1-13	John 11:1-16	Evening Psalm: 48 2 Cor. 3:12-16
Tuesday	Morning Psalm: 52 Ezra 4:7, 11-24	John 11:17-29	Evening Psalm: 125 2 Cor. 3:17-18
Wednesday	Morning Psalm: 121 Ezra 5:1-17	John 11:30-44	Evening Psalm: 33 2 Cor. 4:1-6
Thursday	Morning Psalm: 76 Ezra 6:1-22	John 11:45-54	Evening Psalm: 84 2 Pet. 1:16-21
Friday	Morning Psalm: 56 Ezra 7:11-26	Luke 9:18-27	Evening Psalm: 22 1 Tim. 3:16-4:5
Saturday	Morning Psalm: 27 Mal. 4:1-6	Luke 9:28-36	Evening Psalm: 8 2 Cor. 3:7-18

Transfiguration Sunday (*Last Sunday after Epiphany*)

Sunday	Morning Psalm: 50 2 Kings 2:1-12a	Mark 9:2-9	Evening Psalm: 29 2 Cor. 4:3-6
Monday	Morning Psalm: 2 Ezra 7:27-28; 8:21-36	Matt. 17:1-9	Evening Psalm: 99 2 Cor. 4:7-18
Tuesday	Morning Psalm: 91 Ezra 9:1-15	Matt. 4:1-11	Evening Psalm: 51 2 Cor. 5:1-10
Ash Wednesday	Morning Psalm: 51 Joel 2:1-2, 12-17a	Matt. 6:1-6, 16-21	Evening Psalm: 102 2 Cor. 5:20b-6:10
Thursday	Morning Psalm: 38 Ezra 10:1-17	Luke 18:9-14	Evening Psalm: 32 Titus 1:1-16
Friday	Morning Psalm: 6 Neh. 1:1-11	Luke 9:57-62	Evening Psalm: 39 Titus 2:1-15
Saturday	Morning Psalm: 122 Neh. 2:1-20	Luke 4:1-8	Evening Psalm: 48 Titus 3:1-15

*If this is last Sunday after Epiphany, skip to Transfiguration Sunday.

A Daily Lectionary

Lent 1

Sunday	Morning Psalm: 149 Gen. 9:8-17	Mark 1:9-15	Evening Psalm: 91 1 Pet. 3:18-22
Monday	Morning Psalm: 79 Neh. 4:1-23	Luke 4:9-15	Evening Psalm: 123 1 Pet. 2:20-25
Tuesday	Morning Psalm: 52 Neh. 5:1-19	Luke 4:16-21	Evening Psalm: 120 Rom. 5:1-8
Wednesday	Morning Psalm: 41 Neh. 6:1-19	Luke 4:22-30	Evening Psalm: 55 Gal. 3:2-9
Thursday	Morning Psalm: 119:1-24 Neh. 8:1-18	Matt. 5:17-26	Evening Psalm: 119:25-48 Gal. 3:10-18
Friday	Morning Psalm: 78:1-31 Neh. 9:1-15	Matt. 5:27-37	Evening Psalm: 78:32-72 Rom. 4:1-8
Saturday	Morning Psalm: 106:1-27 Neh. 9:16-25	Mark 8:22-30	Evening Psalm: 106:27-48 Rom. 4:9-15

Lent 2

Sunday	Morning Psalm: 150 Gen. 17:1-10, 15-19	Mark 8:31-38	Evening Psalm: 127 Rom. 4:16-25
Monday	Morning Psalm: 135 Neh. 9:26-38	Matt. 5:38-48	Evening Psalm: 133 Rom. 4:26-31
Tuesday	Morning Psalm: 87 Neh. 12:27-30, 43-47	Matt. 6:1-6	Evening Psalm: 84 Heb. 11:8-12
Wednesday	Morning Psalm: 119:97-120 Neh. 13:4-22	Matt. 6:7-15	Evening Psalm: 119:121-152 Heb. 11:13-19
Thursday	Morning Psalm: 72 Jer. 22:13-22	Matt. 21:12-22	Evening Psalm: 8 1 Cor. 2:1-9
Friday	Morning Psalm: 80 Jer. 23:1-8	Matt. 21:33-43	Evening Psalm: 23 1 Cor. 2:10-16
Saturday	Morning Psalm: 101 Jer. 23:9-15	Mark 11:15-19	Evening Psalm: 35 2 Cor. 13:2-9

Year B

Lent 3

Sunday	Morning Psalm: 103		Evening Psalm: 119:49-72
	Exod. 20:1-17	John 2:13-22	1 Cor. 1:22-25
Monday	Morning Psalm: 129		Evening Psalm: 139
	Jer. 23:16-24	Mark 12:38-44	Rom. 8:18-25
Tuesday	Morning Psalm: 81		Evening Psalm: 82
	Jer. 23:25-32	Luke 12:1-10	Rom. 8:31-39
Wednesday	Morning Psalm: 1		Evening Psalm: 37
	Jer. 24:1-10	Luke 12:11-21	Col. 3:1-17
Thursday	Morning Psalm: 144		Evening Psalm: 8
	Jer. 25:8-17	Luke 12:22-31	1 Pet. 2:4-10
Friday	Morning Psalm: 18:1-19		Evening Psalm: 18:20-50
	Jer. 25:30-38	Luke 12:32-40	1 Pet. 2:11-17
Saturday	Morning Psalm: 56		Evening Psalm: 28
	Jer. 26:1-16	Luke 12:57-13:5	Eph. 1:16-2:3

Lent 4

Sunday	Morning Psalm: 34		Evening Psalm: 74
	2 Chron. 36:14-23	John 3:14-21	Eph. 2:4-10
Monday	Morning Psalm: 83		Evening Psalm: 77
	Lam. 1:1-13	John 8:21-30	Col. 2:8-15
Tuesday	Morning Psalm: 137		Evening Psalm: 4
	Lam. 1:14-22	John 8:31-38	1 Pet. 3:8-12
Wednesday	Morning Psalm: 75		Evening Psalm: 132
	Lam. 2:1-6	John 9:1-7	1 Pet. 3:13-22
Thursday	Morning Psalm: 3		Evening Psalm: 50
	Lam. 2:7-16	John 10:1-6	1 Pet. 4:1-6
Friday	Morning Psalm: 62		Evening Psalm: 42
	Lam. 2:17-22	John 11:55-12:8	Heb. 2:10-18
Saturday	Morning Psalm: 24		Evening Psalm: 88
	Lam. 3:1-18	John 12:9-19	Heb. 5:1-6

A Daily Lectionary

Lent 5

Sunday	Morning Psalm: 119:73-96		Evening Psalm: 126
	Jer. 31:31-34	John 12:20-33	Heb. 5:7-10
Monday	Morning Psalm: 16		Evening Psalm: 33
	Lam. 3:19-39	John 12:32-40	1 Pet. 1:13-21
Tuesday	Morning Psalm: 25		Evening Psalm: 86
	Lam. 3:40-54	John 12:41-48	1 Pet. 1:22-2:3
Wednesday	Morning Psalm: 130		Evening Psalm: 119:153-176
	Lam. 3:55-66	John 12:49-59	Rom. 10:14-21
Thursday	Morning Psalm: 68		Evening Psalm: 113
	Lam. 4:1-10	Mark 13:1-13	Rom. 11:1-12
Friday	Morning Psalm: 114		Evening Psalm: 94
	Lam. 4:11-22	Mark 13:14-27	Rom. 11:13-24
Saturday	Morning Psalm: 9		Evening Psalm: 44
	Lam. 5:1-22	Mark 13:28-37	Rom. 11:25-36

Holy Week
Passion/Palm Sunday

	Morning Psalm: 29		Evening Psalm: 31
	Isa. 50:4-9a	Mark 14:1-15:47	Phil. 2:5-11
		or Mark 11:1-11	
Monday	Morning Psalm: 36		Evening Psalm: 142
	Isa. 42:1-9	John 12:1-11	Heb. 9:11-15
Tuesday	Morning Psalm: 71		Evening Psalm: 143
	Isa. 49:1-7	John 12:20-36	1 Cor. 1:18-31
Wednesday	Morning Psalm: 70		Evening Psalm: 116
	Isa. 50:4-9a	John 13:21-30	Heb. 12:1-3

Maundy Thursday

Morning Psalm: 69:1-15		Evening Psalm: 69:16-36
Exod. 24:3-8	Mark 14:12-26	1 Cor. 10:16-17

Good Friday

Morning Psalm: 22:1-15		Evening Psalm: 22:16-31
Isa. 52:13-53:12	John 18:1-19:42	Heb. 4:14-16; 5:7-9
	or John 19:17-30	

Holy Saturday

Morning Psalm: 89:1-25		Evening Psalm: 89:26-52
Exod. 14:10-15:18	Mark 16:1-8	Rom. 6:3-11

Year B

Easter Sunday

Sunday	Morning Psalm: 118:1-14	Evening Psalm: 118:15-29	
	Acts 10:34-43 or	John 20:1-18 or	1 Cor. 15:1-11 or
	Isa. 25:6-9	Mark 16:1-8	Acts 10:34-43
Monday	Morning Psalm: 150		Evening Psalm: 18:1-19
	Jon. 2:1-9	Mark 16:1-8	Acts 2:14, 22-32
Tuesday	Morning Psalm: 148		Evening Psalm: 18:20-50
	Isa. 30:18-21	Mark 16:9-20	Acts 2:36-41
Wednesday	Morning Psalm: 27		Evening Psalm: 117
	Mic. 7:7-15	Matt. 28:1-16	Acts 3:1-10
Thursday	Morning Psalm: 104		Evening Psalm: 112
	Ezek. 37:1-14	Matt. 28:16-20	Acts 3:11-16
Friday	Morning Psalm: 147		Evening Psalm: 111
	Dan. 12:1-4, 13	Mark 12:18-27	Acts 4:1-12
Saturday	Morning Psalm: 146		Evening Psalm: 20
	Isa. 25:1-9	John 14:8-17	Acts 4:13-21

Easter 2

Sunday	Morning Psalm: 2		Evening Psalm: 26
	Acts 4:32-35	John 20:19-31	1 John 1:1-2:2
Monday	Morning Psalm: 5		Evening Psalm: 15
	Dan. 1:1-21	John 21:1-14	Col. 1:1-14
Tuesday	Morning Psalm: 17		Evening Psalm: 46
	Dan. 2:1-16	John 21:15-19	Col. 1:15-23
Wednesday	Morning Psalm: 36		Evening Psalm: 141
	Dan. 2:17-30	John 21:20-25	Col. 1:24-2:7
Thursday	Morning Psalm: 58		Evening Psalm: 49
	Dan. 2:31-49	Luke 24:1-12	Col. 2:8-23
Friday	Morning Psalm: 12		Evening Psalm: 7
	Dan. 3:1-18	Luke 24:13-27	Col. 3:1-17
Saturday	Morning Psalm: 10		Evening Psalm: 11
	Dan. 3:19-30	Luke 24:28-34	Col. 3:18-4:6

A Daily Lectionary

Easter 3

Sunday	Morning Psalm: 30 Acts 3:12-19	Luke 24:35-48	Evening Psalm: 138 1 John 3:1-7
Monday	Morning Psalm: 96 Dan. 4:1-18	John 20:19-23	Evening Psalm: 98 2 Tim. 1:1-14
Tuesday	Morning Psalm: 109 Dan. 4:19-27	John 20:24-31	Evening Psalm: 90 2 Tim. 1:15-2:13
Wednesday	Morning Psalm: 21 Dan. 4:28-37	Mark 9:38-50	Evening Psalm: 19 2 Tim. 2:14-26
Thursday	Morning Psalm: 121 Dan. 5:1-12	Mark 10:23-31	Evening Psalm: 53 2 Tim. 3:1-17
Friday	Morning Psalm: 80 Dan. 5:13-30	Mark 12:1-11	Evening Psalm: 64 2 Tim. 4:1-8
Saturday	Morning Psalm: 57 Dan. 6:1-15	John 10:1-10	Evening Psalm: 59 2 Tim. 4:9-22

Easter 4

Sunday	Morning Psalm: 100 Acts 4:8-12	John 10:11-18	Evening Psalm: 23 1 John 3:18-24
Monday	Morning Psalm: 54 Dan. 6:16-28	John 10:22-30	Evening Psalm: 93 1 John 1:1-4
Tuesday	Morning Psalm: 43 Dan. 12:1-13	John 10:31-38	Evening Psalm: 13 1 John 1:5-10
Wednesday	Morning Psalm: 65 Ezek. 34:11-16	Matt. 7:1-12	Evening Psalm: 95 1 John 2:1-6
Thursday	Morning Psalm: 40 Deut. 30:15-20	Matt. 7:13-21	Evening Psalm: 131 1 John 2:7-11
Friday	Morning Psalm: 61 Jer. 14:14-18	Matt. 7:22-27	Evening Psalm: 140 1 John 2:12-17
Saturday	Morning Psalm: 63 Isa. 40:9-11	Matt. 7:28-8:4	Evening Psalm: 66 1 John 2:18-23

Year B

Easter 5

Sunday	Morning Psalm: 145 Acts 8:26-40	John 15:1-8	Evening Psalm: 85 1 John 4:7-12
Monday	Morning Psalm: 107:1-22 Song of Sol. 2:1-7	Matt. 8:5-17	Evening Psalm: 34 1 John 2:24-29
Tuesday	Morning Psalm: 45 Song of Sol. 3:1-5	Matt. 8:18-27	Evening Psalm: 107:23-43 1 John 3:1-10
Wednesday	Morning Psalm: 92 Song of Sol. 5:1-8	Matt. 8:28-34	Evening Psalm: 124 1 John 3:11-18
Thursday	Morning Psalm: 108 Song of Sol. 5:9-16	Matt. 9:1-8	Evening Psalm: 125 1 John 3:19-24
Friday	Morning Psalm: 115 Song of Sol. 6:1-10	Matt. 9:9-17	Evening Psalm: 128 1 John 4:1-6
Saturday	Morning Psalm: 99 Song of Sol. 8:1-7	Matt. 9:18-26	Evening Psalm: 103 1 John 4:7-12

Easter 6

Sunday	Morning Psalm: 67 Acts 10:44-48	John 15:9-17	Evening Psalm: 68 1 John 5:1-6
Monday	Morning Psalm: 150 Isa. 63:3-9	Luke 12:13-21	Evening Psalm: 39 1 John 4:13-21
Tuesday	Morning Psalm: 60 Isa. 45:1-8	Matt. 13:1-17	Evening Psalm: 73 1 John 5:1-5
Wednesday	Morning Psalm: 1 Ezek. 1:1-14	Matt. 13:18-23	Evening Psalm: 136 Eph. 1:1-10
Ascension Day	Morning Psalm: 47 Acts 1:1-11	Luke 24:46-53 or Mark 16:9-16, 19-20	Evening Psalm: 105:1-22 Eph. 1:15-23
Friday	Morning Psalm: 105:23-45 Ezek. 1:15-28a	Matt. 22:41-46	Evening Psalm: 110 1 John 5:6-12
Saturday	Morning Psalm: 19 Ezek. 1:28b-3:3	Matt. 28:11-20	Evening Psalm: 14 1 John 5:13-21

A Daily Lectionary

Easter 7

Sunday	Morning Psalm: 97		Evening Psalm: 134
	Acts 1:15-17, 21-26	John 17:11b-19	1 John 5:9-13
Monday	Morning Psalm: 106:1-23		Evening Psalm: 106:24-48
	Ezek. 3:4-17	Luke 10:1-17	2 John 1-13
Tuesday	Morning Psalm: 52		Evening Psalm: 64
	Ezek. 3:17-27	Luke 10:17-24	3 John 1-8
Wednesday	Morning Psalm: 122		Evening Psalm: 137
	Ezek. 4:1-17	Luke 10:25-37	3 John 9-15
Thursday	Morning Psalm: 27		Evening Psalm: 79
	Ezek. 6:1-14	Luke 10:38-42	Rom. 8:1-11
Friday	Morning Psalm: 53		Evening Psalm: 33
	Ezek. 7:1-13	Luke 11:14-23	Rom. 8:12-17
Saturday	Morning Psalm: 119:1-24		Evening Psalm: 74
	Ezek. 7:14-27	John 14:21-29	Rom. 8:18-25

Pentecost Sunday

Sunday	Morning Psalm: 104:24-35		Evening Psalm: 85
	Acts 2:1-21	John 15:26-27	Rom. 8:22-27
Monday	Morning Psalm: 87		Evening Psalm: 104:1-23
	Ezek. 10:1-5, 9-17	John 4:19-26	Rom. 8:26-30
Tuesday	Morning Psalm: 52		Evening Psalm: 105:16-45
	Ezek. 11:14-25	John 11:55-12:8	Rom. 8:31-39
Wednesday	Morning Psalm: 41		Evening Psalm: 105:1-15
	Ezek. 18:1-18	John 12:9-19	Rom. 9:1-18
Thursday	Morning Psalm: 119:1-24		Evening Psalm: 79
	Ezek. 18:21-32	John 12:20-26	Rom. 9:19-33
Friday	Morning Psalm: 119:25-48		Evening Psalm: 74
	Ezek. 24:15-27	John 12:27-36a	Rom. 10:1-13
Saturday	Morning Psalm: 122		Evening Psalm: 84
	Ezek. 43:1-12	John 12:36b-43	Rom. 10:14-21

Year B

Trinity Sunday

Sunday	Morning Psalm: 149		Evening Psalm: 8
	Isa. 6:1-8	John 3:1-17	Rom. 8:12-17
Monday	Morning Psalm: 62		Evening Psalm: 33
	1 Sam. 1:1-20	John 12:44-50	Rom. 11:1-12
Tuesday	Morning Psalm: 75		Evening Psalm: 113
	1 Sam. 1:21-2:11	John 13:1-11	Rom. 11:13-24
Wednesday	Morning Psalm: 53		Evening Psalm: 14
	1 Sam. 2:12-26	John 13:12-20	Rom. 11:25-36
Thursday	Morning Psalm: 41		Evening Psalm: 55
	1 Sam. 2:27-36	John 13:21-30	2 Cor. 1:1-11
Friday	Morning Psalm: 71		Evening Psalm: 40
	1 Sam. 3:1-4:1a	John 13:31-38	2 Cor. 1:12-22
Saturday	Morning Psalm: 78:1-31		Evening Psalm: 78:32-72
	1 Sam. 4:1b-11	John 14:1-7	2 Cor. 1:23-2:17

Proper 4 (*Sunday between May 29 and June 4 if after Trinity Sunday*)*

Sunday	Morning Psalm: 37		Evening Psalm: 117
	1 Sam. 16:1-13	Mark 2:23-3:6	2 Cor. 4:5-12
Monday	Morning Psalm: 27		Evening Psalm: 44
	1 Sam. 4:12-22	John 14:8-14	2 Cor. 3:1-18
Tuesday	Morning Psalm: 135		Evening Psalm: 115
	1 Sam. 5:1-12	John 14:15-24	2 Cor. 4:1-6
Wednesday	Morning Psalm: 131		Evening Psalm: 116
	1 Sam. 6:1-18	John 14:25-31	2 Cor. 4:7-15
Thursday	Morning Psalm: 27		Evening Psalm: 77
	1 Sam. 6:19-7:17	John 15:1-8	2 Cor. 4:16-5:5
Friday	Morning Psalm: 21		Evening Psalm: 10
	1 Sam. 8:1-22	John 15:9-17	2 Cor. 5:6-15
Saturday	Morning Psalm: 72		Evening Psalm: 133
	1 Sam. 9:1-14	John 15:18-27	2 Cor. 5:16-21

If the Sunday between May 24 and 28 follows Trinity Sunday, go back to Proper 3.

A Daily Lectionary

Proper 5 (*Sunday between June 5 and 11 if after Trinity Sunday*)

Sunday	Morning Psalm: 85 1 Sam. 16:14-23	Mark 3:20-35	Evening Psalm: 57 2 Cor. 4:13-5:1
Monday	Morning Psalm: 2 1 Sam. 9:15-10:1	John 16:1-11	Evening Psalm: 70 2 Cor. 6:1-2
Tuesday	Morning Psalm: 30 1 Sam. 10:1-16	John 16:12-24	Evening Psalm: 126 2 Cor. 6:3-13
Wednesday	Morning Psalm: 61 1 Sam. 10:17-27	John 16:25-33	Evening Psalm: 43 2 Cor. 6:14-7:1
Thursday	Morning Psalm: 28 1 Sam. 11:1-15	John 17:1-8	Evening Psalm: 56 2 Cor. 7:2-9
Friday	Morning Psalm: 1 1 Sam. 12:1-6 (7-15), 16-25	John 17:9-17	Evening Psalm: 119:49-72 2 Cor. 7:10-16
Saturday	Morning Psalm: 19 1 Sam. 13:(1-4) 5-18	John 17:18-26	Evening Psalm: 25 2 Cor. 8:1-8

Proper 6 (*Sunday between June 12 and 18 if after Trinity Sunday*)

Sunday	Morning Psalm: 148 2 Sam. 1:1, 17-27	Mark 4:26-34	Evening Psalm: 46 2 Cor. 5:6-10, 14-17
Monday	Morning Psalm: 18:1-24 1 Sam. 13:19-14:15	John 18:1-11	Evening Psalm: 18:25-50 2 Cor. 8:9-16
Tuesday	Morning Psalm: 47 1 Sam. 14:16-30	John 18:12-18	Evening Psalm: 136 2 Cor. 8:17-24
Wednesday	Morning Psalm: 38 1 Sam. 14:31-45	John 18:19-27	Evening Psalm: 39 2 Cor. 9:1-6
Thursday	Morning Psalm: 54 1 Sam. (14:46-52) 15:1-23	John 18:28-40	Evening Psalm: 35 2 Cor. 9:7-15
Friday	Morning Psalm: 17 1 Sam. 15:24-35	John 19:1-11	Evening Psalm: 7 2 Cor. 10:1-6
Saturday	Morning Psalm: 10 1 Sam. 16:1-13	John 19:12-16	Evening Psalm: 13 2 Cor. 10:7-12

Year B

Proper 7 (*Sunday between June 19 and 25 if after Trinity Sunday*)

Sunday	Morning Psalm: 93		Evening Psalm: 48
	2 Sam. 5:1-12	Mark 4:35-41	2 Cor. 5:18-6:2
Monday	Morning Psalm: 22:1-15		Evening Psalm: 22:16-31
	1 Sam. 16:14-7:11	John 19:17-24	2 Cor. 10:13-18
Tuesday	Morning Psalm: 69:1-15		Evening Psalm: 31
	1 Sam. 17:12-30	John 19:25-34	2 Cor. 11:1-6
Wednesday	Morning Psalm: 69:16-36		Evening Psalm: 59
	1 Sam. 17:31-49	John 19:35-42	2 Cor. 11:7-15
Thursday	Morning Psalm: 118		Evening Psalm: 73
	1 Sam. 17:50-18:4	John 20:1-10	2 Cor. 11:16-21a
Friday	Morning Psalm: 45		Evening Psalm: 98
	1 Sam. 18:5-16 (17-27a), 27b-30	John 20:11-18	2 Cor. 11:21b-29
Saturday	Morning Psalm: 83		Evening Psalm: 96
	1 Sam. 19:1-18	John 20:19-23	2 Cor. 11:30-12:6

Proper 8 (*Sunday between June 26 and July 2 inclusive*)

Sunday	Morning Psalm: 24		Evening Psalm: 86
	2 Sam. 6:1-15	Mark 5:21-43	2 Cor. 8:7-15
Monday	Morning Psalm: 3		Evening Psalm: 16
	1 Sam. 19:19-20:17	John 20:24-31	2 Cor. 12:7-11
Tuesday	Morning Psalm: 9		Evening Psalm: 111
	1 Sam. 20:18-42	John 21:1-14	2 Cor. 12:12-18
Wednesday	Morning Psalm: 100		Evening Psalm: 23
	1 Sam. 21:1-15	John 21:15-19	2 Cor. 12:19-21
Thursday	Morning Psalm: 109		Evening Psalm: 141
	1 Sam. 22:1-23	John 21:20-25	2 Cor. 13:1-6
Friday	Morning Psalm: 2		Evening Psalm: 36
	1 Sam. 23:1-23	Mark 1:1-11	2 Cor. 13:7-14
Saturday	Morning Psalm: 12		Evening Psalm: 11
	1 Sam. 23:24-24:22	Mark 1:12-20	Eph. 1:1-10

A Daily Lectionary

Proper 9 (*Sunday between July 3 and 9 inclusive*)

Sunday	Morning Psalm: 89:1-25		Evening Psalm: 89:26-52
	2 Sam. 7:1-7	Mark 6:1-6	2 Cor. 12:1-10
Monday	Morning Psalm: 147		Evening Psalm: 103
	1 Sam. 25:1-22	Mark 1:21-34	Eph. 1:11-15
Tuesday	Morning Psalm: 107:1-22		Evening Psalm: 107:23-43
	1 Sam. 25:23-44	Mark 1:35-45	Eph. 1:16-23
Wednesday	Morning Psalm: 54		Evening Psalm: 42
	1 Sam. 26:1-25	Mark 2:1-12	Eph. 2:1-10
Thursday	Morning Psalm: 120		Evening Psalm: 121
	1 Sam. 27:1-28:2	Mark 2:13-22	Eph. 2:11-23
Friday	Morning Psalm: 144		Evening Psalm: 119:73-96
	1 Sam. 28:3-25	Mark 2:23-3:6	Eph. 3:1-6
Saturday	Morning Psalm: 140		Evening Psalm: 119:49-72
	1 Sam. 29:1-30:10	Mark 3:7-19a	Eph. 3:7-13

Proper 10 (*Sunday between July 10 and 16 inclusive*)

Sunday	Morning Psalm: 149		Evening Psalm: 132
	2 Sam. 7:18-29	Mark 6:7-13	Eph. 1:1-10
Monday	Morning Psalm: 142		Evening Psalm: 138
	1 Sam. 30:11-31	Mark 3:19b-35	Eph. 3:14-21
Tuesday	Morning Psalm: 15		Evening Psalm: 6
	1 Sam. 31:1-13	Mark 4:1-9	Eph. 4:1-6
Wednesday	Morning Psalm: 58		Evening Psalm: 68
	2 Sam. 1:1-16	Mark 4:10-20	Eph. 4:7-16
Thursday	Morning Psalm: 55		Evening Psalm: 127
	2 Sam. 1:17-27	Mark 4:21-32	Eph. 4:17-24
Friday	Morning Psalm: 29		Evening Psalm: 110
	2 Sam. 2:1-17	Mark 4:33-41	Eph. 4:25-32
Saturday	Morning Psalm: 63		Evening Psalm: 64
	2 Sam. 2:18-32	Mark 5:1-13	Eph. 5:1-14

Year B

Proper 11 (*Sunday between July 17 and 23 inclusive*)

Sunday	Morning Psalm: 95		Evening Psalm: 53
	2 Sam. 11:1-15	Mark 6:30-44	Eph. 2:11-22
Monday	Morning Psalm: 101		Evening Psalm: 145
	2 Sam. 3:(1-5) 6-21	Mark 5:14-20	Eph. 5:15-24
Tuesday	Morning Psalm: 67		Evening Psalm: 94
	2 Sam. 3:22-39	Mark 5:21-34	Eph. 5:25-33
Wednesday	Morning Psalm: 88		Evening Psalm: 90
	2 Sam. 4:1-12	Mark 5:35-43	Eph. 6:1-9
Thursday	Morning Psalm: 125		Evening Psalm: 82
	2 Sam. 5:1-16	Mark 6:1-13	Eph. 6:10-17
Friday	Morning Psalm: 129		Evening Psalm: 4
	2 Sam. 5:17-6:11	Mark 6:14-29	Eph. 6:18-24
Saturday	Morning Psalm: 5		Evening Psalm: 84
	2 Sam. 6:12-23	Mark 6:30-44	Acts 21:37-22:5

Proper 12 (*Sunday between July 24 and 30 inclusive*)

Sunday	Morning Psalm: 146		Evening Psalm: 32
	2 Sam. 12:1-14	John 6:1-15	Eph. 3:14-21
Monday	Morning Psalm: 122		Evening Psalm: 84
	2 Sam. 7:1-17	Mark 6:45-52	Acts 22:6-11
Tuesday	Morning Psalm: 72		Evening Psalm: 48
	2 Sam. 7:18-29	Mark 6:53-7:8	Acts 22:12-21
Wednesday	Morning Psalm: 50		Evening Psalm: 119:97-120
	2 Sam. 9:1-13	Mark 7:9-19	Acts 22:22-30
Thursday	Morning Psalm: 76		Evening Psalm: 91
	2 Sam. 10:1-19	Mark 7:20-30	Acts 23:1-5
Friday	Morning Psalm: 92		Evening Psalm: 106:1-23
	2 Sam. 11:1-27	Mark 7:31-37	Acts 23:6-11
Saturday	Morning Psalm: 106:24-48		Evening Psalm: 51
	2 Sam. 12:1-14	Mark 8:1-10	Acts 23:12-30

A Daily Lectionary

Proper 13 (*Sunday between July 31 and August 6 inclusive*)

Sunday	Morning Psalm: 34 2 Sam. 12:15b-24	John 6:24-35	Evening Psalm: 99 Eph. 4:1-6
Monday	Morning Psalm: 119:121-152 2 Sam. 13:1-22	Mark 8:11-21	Evening Psalm: 80 Acts 23:31-24:9
Tuesday	Morning Psalm: 146 2 Sam. 13:23-39	Mark 8:22-30	Evening Psalm: 119:153-176 Acts 24:10-16
Wednesday	Morning Psalm: 66 2 Sam. 14:1-20	Mark 8:31-9:1	Evening Psalm: 124 Acts 24:17-21
Thursday	Morning Psalm: 2 2 Sam. 14:21-33	Mark 9:2-13	Evening Psalm: 97 Acts 24:22-27
Friday	Morning Psalm: 3 2 Sam. 15:1-18	Mark 9:14-29	Evening Psalm: 130 Acts 25:1-12
Saturday	Morning Psalm: 131 2 Sam 15:19-37	Mark 9:30-41	Evening Psalm: 43 Acts 25:13-22

Proper 14 (*Sunday between August 7 and 13 inclusive*)

Sunday	Morning Psalm: 143 2 Sam. 18:1, 5, 9-15	John 6:35, 41-51	Evening Psalm: 117 Eph. 4:25-5:2
Monday	Morning Psalm: 38 2 Sam. 16:1-23	Mark 9:42-50	Evening Psalm: 60 Acts 25:23-26:8
Tuesday	Morning Psalm: 27 2 Sam. 17:1-23	Mark 10:1-12	Evening Psalm: 128 Acts 26:9-18
Wednesday	Morning Psalm: 123 2 Sam. 17:24-18:8	Mark 10:13-22	Evening Psalm: 127 Acts 26:19-23
Thursday	Morning Psalm: 109 2 Sam. 18:9-18	Mark 10:23-31	Evening Psalm: 49 Acts 26:24-32
Friday	Morning Psalm: 2 2 Sam. 18:19-33	Mark 10:32-41	Evening Psalm: 31 Acts 27:1-8
Saturday	Morning Psalm: 15 2 Sam. 19:1-23	Mark 10:42-52	Evening Psalm: 114 Acts 27:9-20

Year B

Proper 15 (*Sunday between August 14 and 20 inclusive*)

Sunday	Morning Psalm: 102		Evening Psalm: 134
	2 Sam. 18:24-33	John 6:51-58	Eph. 5:15-20
Monday	Morning Psalm: 90		Evening Psalm: 118
	2 Sam. 19:24-43	Mark 11:1-11	Acts 27:21-26
Tuesday	Morning Psalm: 122		Evening Psalm: 48
	2 Sam. 21:1-22	Mark 11:12-19	Acts 27:27-32
Wednesday	Morning Psalm: 18:1-24		Evening Psalm: 18:25-50
	2 Sam. 22:1-20	Mark 11:20-26	Acts 27:33-38
Thursday	Morning Psalm: 144		Evening Psalm: 27
	2 Sam. 22:21-51	Mark 11:27-33	Acts 27:39-44
Friday	Morning Psalm: 80		Evening Psalm: 89:26-52
	2 Sam. 23:1-17	Mark 12:1-11	Acts 28:1-10
Saturday	Morning Psalm: 24		Evening Psalm: 103
	2 Sam. 24:1-2 (3-9), 10-25	Mark 12:12-17	Acts 28:11-22

Proper 16 (*Sunday between August 21 and 27 inclusive*)

Sunday	Morning Psalm: 67		Evening Psalm: 105:1-22
	2 Sam. 23:1-7	John 6:55-69	Eph. 5:21-33
Monday	Morning Psalm: 150		Evening Psalm: 105:23-45
	1 Chron. 16:8-22	Mark 12:18-27	Acts 28:23-31
Tuesday	Morning Psalm: 96		Evening Psalm: 29
	1 Chron. 8:23-36	Mark 12:28-34	James 1:1-11
Wednesday	Morning Psalm: 2		Evening Psalm: 132
	1 Chron. 17:1-15	Mark 12:35-44	James 1:12-18
Thursday	Morning Psalm: 46		Evening Psalm: 48
	1 Chron. 17:16-27	Mark 13:1-7	James 1:19-27
Friday	Morning Psalm: 51		Evening Psalm: 32
	1 Chron. 21:1-17	Mark 13:8-13	James 2:1-7
Saturday	Morning Psalm: 87		Evening Psalm: 84
	1 Chron. 21:18-30	Mark 13:14-27	James 2:8-17

A Daily Lectionary

Proper 17 (*Sunday between August 28 and September 3 inclusive*)

Sunday	Morning Psalm: 121 1 Kings 2:1-4, 10-12	Mark 7:1-8, 14-15, 21-23	Evening Psalm: 117 Eph. 6:10-20
Monday	Morning Psalm: 122 1 Chron. 22:1-19	Mark 13:28-37	Evening Psalm: 125 James 2:18-26
Tuesday	Morning Psalm: 149 1 Chron. 29:1-13	Mark 14:1-9	Evening Psalm: 144 James 3:1-5
Wednesday	Morning Psalm: 72 1 Chron. 29:14-25 (26-30)	Mark 14:10-16	Evening Psalm: 39 James 3:6-12
Thursday	Morning Psalm: 121 2 Chron. 20:1-19	Mark 14:17-31	Evening Psalm: 25 James 3:13-18
Friday	Morning Psalm: 63 2 Chron. 20:20-30	Mark 14:32-42	Evening Psalm: 17 James 4:1-6
Saturday	Morning Psalm: 137 2 Chron. 36:11-23	Mark 14:43-52	Evening Psalm: 79 James 4:7-12

Proper 18 (*Sunday between September 4 and 10 inclusive*)

Sunday	Morning Psalm: 119:97-120 Prov. 2:1-8	Mark 7:31-37	Evening Psalm: 119:121-152 James 1:17-27
Monday	Morning Psalm: 1 Prov. 1:1-19	Mark 14:53-65	Evening Psalm: 111 James 4:13-17
Tuesday	Morning Psalm: 19 Prov. 1:20-33	Mark 14:66-72	Evening Psalm: 81 James 5:1-6
Wednesday	Morning Psalm: 119:49-72 Prov. 3:1-12	Mark 15:1-15	Evening Psalm: 119:73-96 James 5:7-12
Thursday	Morning Psalm: 3 Prov. 3:13-26	Mark 15:16-32	Evening Psalm: 119:153-176 James 5:13-20
Friday	Morning Psalm: 36 Prov. 4:1-19	Mark 15:33-39	Evening Psalm: 22 Phil. 1:1-11
Saturday	Morning Psalm: 69:1-18 Prov. 30:1-20	Mark 15:40-47	Evening Psalm: 69:19-36 Phil. 1:12-20

Year B

Proper 19 (*Sunday between September 11 and 17 inclusive*)

Sunday	Morning Psalm: 150		Evening Psalm: 125
	Prov. 22:1-2, 8-9	Mark 8:27-38	James 2:1-5, 8-10, 14-17
Monday	Morning Psalm: 118		Evening Psalm: 97
	Prov. 30:21-33	Mark 16:1-8	Phil. 1:21-27
Tuesday	Morning Psalm: 6		Evening Psalm: 127
	Job 1:1-22	Mark 16:9-20	Phil. 1:27-30
Wednesday	Morning Psalm: 42		Evening Psalm: 43
	Job 2:1-13	Luke 2:41-52	Phil. 2:1-5
Thursday	Morning Psalm: 28		Evening Psalm: 26
	Job 3:1-26	Luke 3:1-14	Phil. 2:6-13
Friday	Morning Psalm: 71		Evening Psalm: 62
	Job 4:1-6, 12-21	Luke 3:15-22	Phil. 2:14-18
Saturday	Morning Psalm: 65		Evening Psalm: 113
	Job 4:1, 5:1-17 (18-27)	Luke 4:1-13	Phil. 2:19-30

Proper 20 (*Sunday between September 18 and 24 inclusive*)

Sunday	Morning Psalm: 131		Evening Psalm: 27
	Job 28:20-28	Mark 9:30-37	James 3:13-18
Monday	Morning Psalm: 38		Evening Psalm: 88
	Job 6:1-13	Luke 4:14-30	Phil. 3:1-7
Tuesday	Morning Psalm: 17		Evening Psalm: 7
	Job 6:14-30	Luke 4:31-37	Phil. 3:8-11
Wednesday	Morning Psalm: 40		Evening Psalm: 8
	Job 7:1-21	Luke 4:38-44	Phil. 3:12-21
Thursday	Morning Psalm: 129		Evening Psalm: 9
	Job 8:1-22	Luke 5:1-11	Phil. 4:1-7
Friday	Morning Psalm: 148		Evening Psalm: 143
	Job 9:1-15	Luke 5:12-26	Phil. 4:8-13
Saturday	Morning Psalm: 45		Evening Psalm: 109
	Job 9:16-35	Luke 5:27-39	Phil. 4:14-23

A Daily Lectionary

Proper 21 (*Sunday between September 25 and October 1 inclusive*)

Sunday	Morning Psalm: 102 Job 42:1-6	Mark 9:38-50	Evening Psalm: 139 James 4:13-17; 5:7-11
Monday	Morning Psalm: 57 Job 10:1-22	Luke 6:1-11	Evening Psalm: 13 Philem. 1-14
Tuesday	Morning Psalm: 37 Job 11:1-20	Luke 6:12-26	Evening Psalm: 10 Philem. 15-25
Wednesday	Morning Psalm: 107:1-22 Job 12:1-25	Luke 6:27-38	Evening Psalm: 107:23-43 Heb. 1:1-7
Thursday	Morning Psalm: 55 Job 13:1-12	Luke 6:39-49	Evening Psalm: 44 Heb. 1:8-14
Friday	Morning Psalm: 144 Job 13:13-28	Luke 7:1-17	Evening Psalm: 8 Heb. 2:1-9
Saturday	Morning Psalm: 92 Job 14:1-22	Luke 7:18-27	Evening Psalm: 73 Heb. 2:10-18

Proper 22 (*Sunday between October 2 and 8 inclusive*)

Sunday	Morning Psalm: 147 Gen. 2:18-24	Mark 10:2-16	Evening Psalm: 128 Heb. 1:1-4; 2:9-11
Monday	Morning Psalm: 63 Job 16:1; 17:1-16	Luke 7:28-35	Evening Psalm: 11 Heb. 3:1-6
Tuesday	Morning Psalm: 85 Job 19:1-7, 14-27	Luke 7:36-50	Evening Psalm: 130 Heb. 3:7-14
Wednesday	Morning Psalm: 1 Job 22:1-4, 21-23:7	Luke 8:1-15	Evening Psalm: 68 Heb. 3:15-19
Thursday	Morning Psalm: 98 Job 25:1-6; 27:1-6	Luke 8:16-25	Evening Psalm: 95 Heb. 4:1-7
Friday	Morning Psalm: 103 Job 29:1-20	Luke 8:26-39	Evening Psalm: 33 Heb. 4:8-13
Saturday	Morning Psalm: 140 Job 30:1-15	Luke 8:40-56	Evening Psalm: 110 Heb. 4:14-5:6

Year B

Proper 23 (*Sunday between October 9 and 15 inclusive*)

Sunday	Morning Psalm: 134		Evening Psalm: 90
	Gen. 3:8-19	Mark 10:17-30	Heb. 4:1-3, 9-13
Monday	Morning Psalm: 24		Evening Psalm: 15
	Job 30:16-31	Luke 9:1-17	Heb. 5:7-14
Tuesday	Morning Psalm: 65		Evening Psalm: 112
	Job 31:1-23	Luke 9:18-27	Heb. 6:1-8
Wednesday	Morning Psalm: 21		Evening Psalm: 20
	Job 31:24-40	Luke 9:28-36	Heb. 6:9-12
Thursday	Morning Psalm: 52		Evening Psalm: 56
	Job 32:1-10, 20-33:1, 19-33	Luke 9:37-50	Heb. 6:13-20
Friday	Morning Psalm: 104:1-13		Evening Psalm: 104:14-35
	Job 38:1-17	Luke 9:51-62	Heb. 7:1-10
Saturday	Morning Psalm: 135		Evening Psalm: 136
	Job 38:1, 18-41	Luke 10:1-17	Heb. 7:11-19

Proper 24 (*Sunday between October 16 and 22 inclusive*)

Sunday	Morning Psalm: 123		Evening Psalm: 35
	Isa. 53:7-12	Mark 10:35-45	Heb. 4:14-16
Monday	Morning Psalm: 148		Evening Psalm: 74
	Job 38:1; 39:1-12	Luke 10:17-24	Heb. 7:20-28
Tuesday	Morning Psalm: 101		Evening Psalm: 116
	Job 38:1; 39:13-30	Luke 10:25-37	Heb. 8:1-5
Wednesday	Morning Psalm: 50		Evening Psalm: 37
	Job 40:1-24	Luke 10:38-42	Heb. 8:6-13
Thursday	Morning Psalm: 75		Evening Psalm: 141
	Job 40:1; 41:1-11	Luke 11:1-13	Heb. 9:1-10
Friday	Morning Psalm: 70		Evening Psalm: 86
	Job 42:1-17	Luke 11:14-26	Heb. 9:11-14
Saturday	Morning Psalm: 133		Evening Psalm: 49
	Job 28:1-28	Luke 11:27-36	Heb. 9:15-22

A Daily Lectionary

Proper 25 (*Sunday between October 23 and 29 inclusive*)

Sunday	Morning Psalm: 106:1-23		Evening Psalm: 126
	Jer. 31:7-9	Mark 10:46-52	Heb. 5:1-6
Monday	Morning Psalm: 106:24-48		Evening Psalm: 138
	Jer. 31:27-37	Luke 11:37-52	Heb. 9:23-28
Tuesday	Morning Psalm: 124		Evening Psalm: 94
	Jer. 32:1-16	Luke 11:53-12:12	Heb. 10:1-10
Wednesday	Morning Psalm: 76		Evening Psalm: 80
	Jer. 32:17-30	Luke 12:13-31	Heb. 10:11-18
Thursday	Morning Psalm: 78:1-31		Evening Psalm: 78:32-72
	Jer. 33:10-16	Luke 12:32-48	Heb. 10:19-25
Friday	Morning Psalm: 18:1-24		Evening Psalm: 18:25-50
	Jer. 34:8-22	Luke 12:49-59	Heb. 10:26-31
Saturday	Morning Psalm: 58		Evening Psalm: 91
	Jer. 35:1-19	Luke 13:1-9	Heb. 10:32-39

Proper 26 (*Sunday between October 30 and November 5 inclusive*)

Sunday	Morning Psalm: 119:1-24		Evening Psalm: 119:25-48
	Deut. 6:1-9	Mark 12:28-34	Heb. 7:23-28
Monday	Morning Psalm: 16		Evening Psalm: 4
	Jer. 36:1-10	Luke 13:10-17	1 Tim. 1:1-11
Tuesday	Morning Psalm: 5		Evening Psalm: 12
	Jer. 36:11-26	Luke 13:18-30	1 Tim. 1:12-20
Wednesday	Morning Psalm: 120		Evening Psalm: 64
	Jer. 36:27-37:2	Luke 13:31-35	1 Tim. 2:1-7
Thursday	Morning Psalm: 142		Evening Psalm: 59
	Jer. 37:3-21	Luke 14:1-11	1 Tim. 2:8-15
Friday	Morning Psalm: 30		Evening Psalm: 34
	Jer. 38:1-13	Luke 14:12-24	1 Tim. 3:1-7
Saturday	Morning Psalm: 41		Evening Psalm: 31
	Jer. 38:14-28	Luke 14:25-35	1 Tim. 3:8-16

Year B

Proper 27 (*Sunday between November 6 and 12 inclusive*)

Day	Morning	Gospel	Evening
Sunday	Morning Psalm: 146 1 Kings 17:8-16	Mark 12:38-44	Evening Psalm: 47 Heb. 9:24-28
Monday	Morning Psalm: 83 Jer. 39:1-18	Luke 15:1-10	Evening Psalm: 60 1 Tim. 4:1-6
Tuesday	Morning Psalm: 53 Jer. 44:1-14	Luke 15:11-32	Evening Psalm: 77 1 Tim. 4:7-16
Wednesday	Morning Psalm: 37 Lam. 1:1-12	Luke 16:1-9	Evening Psalm: 49 1 Tim. 5:1-8
Thursday	Morning Psalm: 89:1-21 Lam. 2:1-15	Luke 16:19-31	Evening Psalm: 82 1 Tim. 5:9-16
Friday	Morning Psalm: 89:22-52 Ezra 1:1-11	Luke 16:10-18	Evening Psalm: 14 1 Tim. 5:17-24
Saturday	Morning Psalm: 108 Ezra 3:1-13	Luke 17:1-10	Evening Psalm: 114 1 Tim. 6:1-5

Proper 28 (*Sunday between November 13 and 19 inclusive*)

Day	Morning	Gospel	Evening
Sunday	Morning Psalm: 145 Dan. 7:9-14	Mark 13:24-32	Evening Psalm: 99 Heb. 10:11-18
Monday	Morning Psalm: 54 Ezra 4:1-24	Luke:17:11-19	Evening Psalm: 115 1 Tim. 6:6-12
Tuesday	Morning Psalm: 61 Ezra 5:1-17	Luke 17:20-37	Evening Psalm: 87 1 Tim. 6:13-21
Wednesday	Morning Psalm: 122 Ezra 6:1-22	Luke 18:1-8	Evening Psalm: 66 Phil. 2:1-11
Thursday	Morning Psalm: 50 Ezra 7:(1-10) 11-26	Luke 18:9-14	Evening Psalm: 15 1 Cor. 3:10-13
Friday	Morning Psalm: 22:1-18 Ezra 7:27-28; 8:21-36	Luke 23:1-12	Evening Psalm: 22:19-31 Eph. 1:3-14
Saturday	Morning Psalm: 69:1-18 Ezra 9:1-15	Luke 23:35-43	Evening Psalm: 69:19-36 Eph. 1:15-23

A Daily Lectionary

Christ the King Sunday

Sunday	Morning Psalm: 93 Jer. 23:1-6	John 18:33-37	Evening Psalm: 100 Rev. 1:4b-8
Monday	Morning Psalm: 24 Ezra 10:1-17	Luke 18:15-30	Evening Psalm: 27 Rom. 15:7-13
Tuesday	Morning Psalm: 31 Neh. 9:1-25	Luke 18:31-43	Evening Psalm: 36 1 Thess. 1:1-5
Wednesday	Morning Psalm: 106:1-23 Neh. 9:26-38	Luke 19:1-10	Evening Psalm: 106:24-48 1 Thess. 1:6-12
Thursday	Morning Psalm: 80 Jer. 3:15-18	Luke 19:11-27	Evening Psalm: 23 1 Thess. 2:1-12
Friday	Morning Psalm: 25 Jer. 4:1-4	Luke 19:28-40	Evening Psalm: 85 1 Thess. 2:13-20
Saturday	Morning Psalm: 84 Jer. 23:1-9	Luke 19:41-48	Evening Psalm: 48 1 Thess. 3:1-9

7
YEAR C

Advent 1

Sunday	Morning Psalm: 25 Jer. 33:14-16	Luke 21:25-36	Evening Psalm: 98 1 Thess. 3:9-13
Monday	Morning Psalm: 89:1-22 Jer. 33:19-26	Luke 21:10-24	Evening Psalm: 89:23-52 1 Thess. 4:1-8
Tuesday	Morning Psalm: 149 Isa. 42:5-9	Mark 13:14-23	Evening Psalm: 115 1 Thess. 4:9-18
Wednesday	Morning Psalm: 82 Mal. 1:1-5	Mark 13:24-37	Evening Psalm: 34 1 Thess. 5:1-11
Thursday	Morning Psalm: 50 Mal. 1:6-14	Mark 1:1-8	Evening Psalm: 40 1 Thess. 5:12-28
Friday	Morning Psalm: 119:1-24 Mal. 2:1-9	Luke 1:57-66	Evening Psalm: 110 Rev. 1:4-8
Saturday	Morning Psalm: 106:1-23 Mal. 2:10-17	Luke 1:67-80	Evening Psalm: 106:24-48 1 John 1:1-4

Advent 2

Sunday	Morning Psalm: 150 Mal. 3:1-4	Luke 3:1-6	Evening Psalm: 126 Phil. 1:3-11
Monday	Morning Psalm: 78:1-31 Mal. 3:6-12	John 3:22-36	Evening Psalm: 78:32-72 1 Cor. 1:10-17
Tuesday	Morning Psalm: 32 Mal. 3:13-18	Matt. 3:1-6	Evening Psalm: 73 2 Thess. 2:1-12
Wednesday	Morning Psalm: 1 Mal. 4:1-6	Matt. 3:7-12	Evening Psalm: 68 2 Thess. 2:13-3:5
Thursday	Morning Psalm: 12 Amos 2:1-8	John 1:6-13	Evening Psalm: 10 James 5:7-12
Friday	Morning Psalm: 52 Amos 2:9-16	John 1:19-28	Evening Psalm: 81 1 Tim. 1:3-11
Saturday	Morning Psalm: 14 Amos 3:1-11	Matt. 23:23-28	Evening Psalm: 19 1 Tim. 1:12-17

A Daily Lectionary

Advent 3

Sunday	Morning Psalm: 19 Zeph. 3:14-20	Luke 3:7-18	Evening Psalm: 117 Phil. 4:4-9
Monday	Morning Psalm: 37:1-22 Amos 3:12-4:5	Matt. 23:29-39	Evening Psalm: 32:32-72 Rom. 12:1-8
Tuesday	Morning Psalm: 58 Amos 4:6-13	Matt. 12:30-37	Evening Psalm: 53 Rom. 2:3-11
Wednesday	Morning Psalm: 75 Amos 5:1-17	Matt. 12:39-45	Evening Psalm: 79 Heb. 9:11-22
Thursday	Morning Psalm: 76 Amos 5:18-27	Matt. 14:1-12	Evening Psalm: 74 Rom. 8:1-6
Friday	Morning Psalm: 83 Amos 6:1-14	Luke 1:5-25	Evening Psalm: 51 Titus 1:11-15
Saturday	Morning Psalm: 92 Amos 7:1-9	Luke 1:26-38	Evening Psalm: 94 Rev. 7:9-17

Advent 4*

Sunday	Morning Psalm: 80 Mic. 5:2-5a	Luke 1:39-55	Evening Psalm: 40 Heb. 10:5-10
Monday	Morning Psalm: 97 Amos 7:10-17	Matt. 1:1-17	Evening Psalm: 110 Heb. 10:11-18
Tuesday	Morning Psalm: 101 Amos 8:1-14	Matt. 1:18-25	Evening Psalm: 119:49-72 Titus 2:1-10
Wednesday	Morning Psalm: 137 Amos 9:1-10	John 1:9-18	Evening Psalm: 139 Titus 2:11-3:7
Thursday	Morning Psalm: 132 Amos 9:9-15	John 5:30-47	Evening Psalm: 65 Gal. 3:1-14
Friday	Morning Psalm: 89:1-22 2 Sam. 7:1-17	John 6:35-51	Evening Psalm: 48 Gal. 3:15-22
Saturday	Morning Psalm: 89:23-52 2 Sam. 7:18-29	John 12:44-50	Evening Psalm: 44 Gal. 3:23-4:7

Christmas Eve

	Morning Psalm: 96 Isa. 9:2-7	Luke 2:1-20	Evening Psalm: 85 Titus 2:11-14

*Skip to Christmas Eve lesson on Christmas Eve.

Year C

Christmas Day

	Morning Psalm: 148		Evening Psalm: 8
	Isa. 62:6-7, 10-12 or	Luke 2:8-20 or	Titus 3:4-7 or
	Isa. 52:7-10	John 1:1-14	Heb. 1:1-12
Dec. 26	Morning Psalm: 130		Evening Psalm: 27
	2 Chron. 24:17-22	Acts. 7:55-8:8	Acts 6:1-7
Dec. 27	Morning Psalm: 119:97-120	Evening Psalm: 119:121-152	
	Prov. 8:22-30	John 13:2-20	1 John 5:1-12
Dec. 28	Morning Psalm: 56		Evening Psalm: 59
	Isa. 49:13-23	Matt. 18:1-14	1 John 4:7-16
Dec. 29	Morning Psalm: 18:1-24		Evening Psalm: 111
	2 Sam. 23:13-17b	John 2:1-11	2 John 1-3
Dec. 30	Morning Psalm: 61		Evening Psalm: 18:25-50
	1 Kings 17:17-24	John 4:46-54	3 John 1-15
Dec. 31	Morning Psalm: 90		Evening Psalm: 31
	1 Kings 3:5-14	John 5:1-15	James 4:13-17; 5:7-11

1st Sunday after Christmas*

	Morning Psalm: 150		Evening Psalm: 90
	1 Sam. 2:18-20, 26	Luke 2:41-52	Col. 3:12-17
Jan. 1	Morning Psalm: 67		Evening Psalm: 121
	Isa. 49:1-10	Luke 14:16-24	Eph. 3:1-10
Jan. 2	Morning Psalm: 69:1-21	Evening Psalm: 69:13-36	
	1 Kings 19:1-8	John 6:1-14	Eph. 4:1-16
Jan. 3	Morning Psalm: 46		Evening Psalm: 77
	1 Kings 19:9-18	John 6:15-27	Eph. 4:17-32
Jan. 4	Morning Psalm: 66		Evening Psalm: 114
	Josh. 3:14-4:7	John 9:1-12, 35-38	Eph. 5:1-20
Jan. 5	Morning Psalm: 88		Evening Psalm: 142
	Jon. 2:2-9	John 11:17-27, 38-44	Eph. 6:10-20

2nd Sunday after Christmas**

	Morning Psalm: 147	Evening Psalm: 119:153-176
	Jer. 31:7-14	John 1:1-18	Eph. 1:3-6, 15-18

When a Sunday lesson coincides with a dated lesson, the Sunday lesson should be read.

**If this is Epiphany, skip to Epiphany reading. This lesson is not read during years in which only one Sunday falls between Christmas and Epiphany.*

A Daily Lectionary

Epiphany	Morning Psalm: 72		Evening Psalm: 48
	Isa. 60:1-6	Matt. 2:1-12	Eph. 3:1-12
Jan. 7	Morning Psalm: 104:1-18		Evening Psalm: 104:19-35
	Deut. 8:1-3	John 6:30-33, 48-51	Col. 1:1-14
Jan. 8	Morning Psalm: 105:1-22		Evening Psalm: 105:23-45
	Exod. 17:1-7	John 7:37-52	Col. 1:15-23
Jan. 9	Morning Psalm: 108		Evening Psalm: 145
	Isa. 45:14-19	John 8:12-19	Col. 1:24-2:7
Jan. 10	Morning Psalm: 100		Evening Psalm: 23
	Jer. 23:1-8	John 10:7-17	Col. 2:8-23
Jan. 11	Morning Psalm: 103		Evening Psalm: 15
	Isa. 55:3-9	John 14:6-14	Col. 3:1-7
Jan. 12	Morning Psalm: 146		Evening Psalm: 127
	Gen. 49:1-2, 8-12	John 15:1-16	Col. 3:18-4:6

1st Sunday after Epiphany*

Sunday	Morning Psalm: 2		Evening Psalm: 29
	Isa. 61:1-4	Luke 3:15-17, 21-22	Acts 8:14-17
Monday	Morning Psalm: 5		Evening Psalm: 134
	Gen. 1:1-2:3	Luke 2:21-32	Acts 10:34-43
Tuesday	Morning Psalm: 24		Evening Psalm: 136
	Gen. 2:4-9	Luke 2:33-40	Acts 11:1-18
Wednesday	Morning Psalm: 38		Evening Psalm: 6
	Gen. 3:1-24	Luke 7:1-10	Eph. 2:11-22
Thursday	Morning Psalm: 28		Evening Psalm: 91
	Gen. 4:1-16	Luke 7:11-17	Rom. 3:1-11
Friday	Morning Psalm: 62		Evening Psalm: 11
	Gen. 4:17-26	Luke 7:18-23	Rom. 9:1-5
Saturday	Morning Psalm: 109		Evening Psalm: 49
	Gen. 6:1-8	Luke 7:24-35	Rom. 12:1-8

*Begin this week of readings on the first Sunday after Epiphany, skipping any dated material necessary.

Year C

2nd Sunday after Epiphany

Sunday	Morning Psalm: 45 Isa. 62:1-5	John 2:1-11	Evening Psalm: 36 1 Cor. 12:1-11
Monday	Morning Psalm: 41 Gen. 6:9-22	John 4:1-15	Evening Psalm: 26 Eph. 4:1-8
Tuesday	Morning Psalm: 93 Gen. 7:1-10, 17-24	John 4:16-30	Evening Psalm: 64 2 Cor. 4:7-15
Wednesday	Morning Psalm: 16 Gen. 8:6-22	John 4:31-45	Evening Psalm: 20 Gal. 3:2-9
Thursday	Morning Psalm: 17 Gen. 9:1-17	Matt. 4:1-11	Evening Psalm: 91 1 John 3:19-24
Friday	Morning Psalm: 102 Gen. 9:18-29	Matt. 4:12-17	Evening Psalm: 7 1 John 4:1-6
Saturday	Morning Psalm: 95 Gen. 11:1-9	Matt. 4:18-25	Evening Psalm: 39 1 John 4:13-21

3rd Sunday after Epiphany

Sunday	Morning Psalm: 19 Neh. 8:1-4a, 5-6, 8-10	Luke 4:14-21	Evening Psalm: 138 1 Cor. 12:12-30
Monday	Morning Psalm: 123 Gen. 11:27-12:9	Matt. 5:1-10	Evening Psalm: 112 1 John 5:6-12
Tuesday	Morning Psalm: 140 Gen. 12:9-13:1	Matt. 5:11-16	Evening Psalm: 55 1 Thess. 5:12-22
Wednesday	Morning Psalm: 133 Gen. 13:2-18	Matt. 5:17-20	Evening Psalm: 42 Rom. 8:2-11
Thursday	Morning Psalm: 54 Gen. 14:8-24	Matt. 5:21-26	Evening Psalm: 110 James 1:19-27
Friday	Morning Psalm: 30 Gen. 15:1-11, 17-21	Matt. 5:27-37	Evening Psalm: 125 1 Pet. 4:7-11
Saturday	Morning Psalm: 63 Gen. 16:1-14	Matt. 5:38-48	Evening Psalm: 60 2 John 4-11

A Daily Lectionary

4th Sunday after Epiphany*

Sunday	Morning Psalm: 71 Jer. 1:4-10	Luke 4:21-30	Evening Psalm: 33 1 Cor. 13:1-13
Monday	Morning Psalm: 144 Gen. 16:15-17:14	Matt. 6:1-6, 16-18	Evening Psalm: 4 3 John 1-8
Tuesday	Morning Psalm: 131 Gen. 17:15-27	Matt. 6:7-15	Evening Psalm: 43 1 Cor. 10:1-13
Wednesday	Morning Psalm: 107:1-22 Gen. 18:1-16	Matt. 6:19-24	Evening Psalm: 113 1 Cor. 10:14-22
Thursday	Morning Psalm: 107:23-43 Gen. 18:16-33	Matt. 6:25-34	Evening Psalm: 141 1 Cor. 10:23-11:2
Friday	Morning Psalm: 3 Gen. 19:1-17, 24-29	Matt. 7:1-12	Evening Psalm: 70 1 Cor. 11:3-16
Saturday	Morning Psalm: 24 Gen. 21:1-21	Matt. 7:13-21	Evening Psalm: 15 1 Cor. 11:17-22

5th Sunday after Epiphany*

Sunday	Morning Psalm: 57 Isa. 61:1-8 (9-13)	Luke 5:1-11	Evening Psalm: 118 1 Cor. 15:1-11
Monday	Morning Psalm: 21 Gen. 22:1-18	Matt. 7:22-27	Evening Psalm: 31 1 Cor. 11:23-26
Tuesday	Morning Psalm: 122 Gen. 23:1-20	Matt. 7:28-8:4	Evening Psalm: 84 1 Cor. 11:27-34
Wednesday	Morning Psalm: 143 Gen. 24:1-27	Matt. 8:5-17	Evening Psalm: 86 1 Cor. 12:1-11
Thursday	Morning Psalm: 47 Gen. 24:28-38, 50-51	Matt. 8:18-27	Evening Psalm: 124 1 Cor. 12:12-26
Friday	Morning Psalm: 35 Gen. 24:50-67	Matt. 8:28-34	Evening Psalm: 13 1 Cor. 12:27-31
Saturday	Morning Psalm: 87 Gen. 25:19-34	Matt. 9:1-8	Evening Psalm: 129 1 Cor. 13:1-13

If this is last Sunday after Epiphany, skip to Transfiguration Sunday.

Year C

Proper 1 (*6th Sunday after Epiphany*)*

Sunday	Morning Psalm: 135		Evening Psalm: 116
	Jer. 17:5-10	Luke 6:17-26	1 Cor. 15:12-20
Monday	Morning Psalm: 50		Evening Psalm: 85
	Gen. 26:1-6, 12-22	Matt. 9:9-17	1 Cor. 14:1-5
Tuesday	Morning Psalm: 147		Evening Psalm: 30
	Gen. 27:1-29	Matt. 9:18-26	1 Cor. 14:6-12
Wednesday	Morning Psalm: 146		Evening Psalm: 145
	Gen. 27:30-45	Matt. 9:27-34	1 Cor. 14:13-19
Thursday	Morning Psalm: 100		Evening Psalm: 23
	Gen. 27:46-28:4, 10-22	Matt. 9:35-10:4	1 Cor. 14:20-25
Friday	Morning Psalm: 22		Evening Psalm: 16
	Gen. 29:1-20	Matt. 10:5-15	1 Cor. 14:26-32
Saturday	Morning Psalm: 69:1-21		Evening Psalm: 69:22-36
	Gen. 29:20-35	Matt. 10:16-23	1 Cor. 14:33-39

Proper 2 (*7th Sunday after Epiphany*)*

Sunday	Morning Psalm: 150		Evening Psalm: 134
	Gen. 45:3-11, 15	Luke 6:27-38	1 Cor. 15:35-38, 42-50
Monday	Morning Psalm: 70		Evening Psalm: 92
	Gen. 30:1-24	Matt. 10:24-33	1 Cor. 15:1-11
Tuesday	Morning Psalm: 99		Evening Psalm: 97
	Gen. 31:1-24	Matt. 10:34-42	1 Cor. 15:12-19
Wednesday	Morning Psalm: 37		Evening Psalm: 124
	Gen. 31:25-50	Matt. 11:1-6	1 Cor. 15:20-25
Thursday	Morning Psalm: 51		Evening Psalm: 133
	Gen. 32:3-21	Matt. 11:7-15	1 Cor. 15:29-34
Friday	Morning Psalm: 38		Evening Psalm: 139
	Gen. 32:22-33:17	Matt. 11:16-24	1 Cor. 15:35-44
Saturday	Morning Psalm: 131		Evening Psalm: 105:1-22
	Gen. 35:1-20	Matt. 11:25-30	1 Cor. 15:45-50

If this is last Sunday after Epiphany, skip to Transfiguration Sunday.

A Daily Lectionary

Proper 3 (*8th Sunday after Epiphany*)*

Sunday	Morning Psalm: 135		Evening Psalm: 42
	Eccles. 27:4-7 or	Luke 6:39-49	1 Cor. 15:51-58
	Isa. 55:10-13		
Monday	Morning Psalm: 41		Evening Psalm: 112
	Judg. 2:1-5, 11-23	Matt. 12:1-14	1 Cor. 16:1-9
Tuesday	Morning Psalm: 108		Evening Psalm: 124
	Judg. 3:12-30	Matt. 12:15-21	1 Cor. 16:10-24
Wednesday	Morning Psalm: 2		Evening Psalm: 83
	Judg. 4:4-23	Matt. 12:22-32	2 Cor. 4:7-18
Thursday	Morning Psalm: 27		Evening Psalm: 68
	Judg. 5:1-18	Matt. 12:33-42	2 Cor. 5:1-10
Friday	Morning Psalm: 18:1-24		Evening Psalm: 18:25-50
	Judg. 5:19-31	Matt. 12:43-50	2 Pet. 1:16-21
Saturday	Morning Psalm: 119:1-24		Evening Psalm: 119:25-48
	Deut. 6:1-9	John 12:24-32	Heb. 12:18-29

Transfiguration Sunday (*Last Sunday after Epiphany*)

Sunday	Morning Psalm: 2		Evening Psalm: 99
	Exod. 34:29-35	Luke 9:28-36	2 Cor. 3:12-4:2
Monday	Morning Psalm: 70		Evening Psalm: 44
	Judg. 6:1-24	John 18:15-18, 25-27	Heb. 1:1-14
Tuesday	Morning Psalm: 16		Evening Psalm: 59
	Judg. 6:25-40	John 18:28-30	Heb. 2:1-10

Ash Wednesday

	Morning Psalm: 38		Evening Psalm: 51
	Joel 2:1-2, 12-17a	Matt. 6:1-6, 16	2 Cor. 5:20b-6:10
Thursday	Morning Psalm: 144		Evening Psalm: 124
	Judg. 7:1-18	John 17:1-8	Heb. 12:1-8
Friday	Morning Psalm: 18:1-24		Evening Psalm: 18:25-50
	Judg. 7:19-8:12	John 17:9-19	Heb. 12:9-17
Saturday	Morning Psalm: 97		Evening Psalm: 99
	Judg. 8:22-35	John 17:20-26	Heb. 12:25-29

*If this is last Sunday after Epiphany, skip to Transfiguration Sunday.

Year C

Lent 1

Sunday	Morning Psalm: 130 Deut. 26:1-11	Luke 4:1-13	Evening Psalm: 117 Rom. 10:8b-13
Monday	Morning Psalm: 5 Judg. 9:1-21	Mark 1:1-13	Evening Psalm: 11 Heb. 2:11-18
Tuesday	Morning Psalm: 30 Judg. 9:22-25, 50-57	Mark 1:14-28	Evening Psalm: 95 Heb. 3:1-11
Wednesday	Morning Psalm: 88 Judg. 11:1-11	Mark 1:29-45	Evening Psalm: 6 Heb. 3:12-19
Thursday	Morning Psalm: 45 Judg. 11:29-40	Mark 2:1-12	Evening Psalm: 39 Heb. 4:1-10
Friday	Morning Psalm: 63 Judg. 12:1-7	Mark 2:13-22	Evening Psalm: 32 Heb. 4:11-16
Saturday	Morning Psalm: 50 Judg. 13:1-14	Mark 2:23-3:6	Evening Psalm: 128 Heb. 5:1-10

Lent 2

Sunday	Morning Psalm: 149 Gen. 15:1-12, 17-18	Luke 13:31-35	Evening Psalm: 33 Phil. 3:17-4:1
Monday	Morning Psalm: 52 Judg. 13:15-24	Mark 3:7-19a	Evening Psalm: 127 Phil. 4:8-13
Tuesday	Morning Psalm: 3 Judg. 14:1-19	Mark 3:19b-35	Evening Psalm: 76 2 Thess. 3:6-13
Wednesday	Morning Psalm: 65 Judg. 14:20-15:20	Mark 4:1-20	Evening Psalm: 119:1-24 Phil. 1:19b-26
Thursday	Morning Psalm: 107:1-22 Judg. 16:1-22	Mark 4:21-34	Evening Psalm: 107:23-43 Phil. 1:27-2:2
Friday	Morning Psalm: 29 Judg. 16:23-31	Mark 4:35-41	Evening Psalm: 93 Gal. 3:23-29
Saturday	Morning Psalm: 28 Judg. 17:1-13	Mark 5:1-20	Evening Psalm: 40 1 Pet. 2:1-10

A Daily Lectionary

Lent 3

Sunday	Morning Psalm: 103		Evening Psalm: 95
	Exod. 3:1-15	Luke 13:1-9	1 Cor. 10:1-13
Monday	Morning Psalm: 67		Evening Psalm: 61
	Judg. 18:1-15	Mark 5:21-43	Rom. 13:8-14
Tuesday	Morning Psalm: 56		Evening Psalm: 128
	Judg. 18:16-31	Mark 6:1-13	Rom. 14:1-12
Wednesday	Morning Psalm: 43		Evening Psalm: 35
	Eccles. 1:1-11	Mark 6:13-29	2 Tim. 2:8-17
Thursday	Morning Psalm: 119:25-48		Evening Psalm: 119:49-72
	Eccles. 1:12-18	Mark 6:30-46	Rom. 6:2-11
Friday	Morning Psalm: 119:73-96		Evening Psalm: 115
	Eccles. 2:1-16	Mark 6:47-56	Col. 1:11-20
Saturday	Morning Psalm: 119:97-120		Evening Psalm: 49
	Eccles. 2:16-26	Mark 7:1-23	Col. 3:1-11

Lent 4

Sunday	Morning Psalm: 145		Evening Psalm: 23
	Josh. 5:9-12	Luke 15:1-3, 11-32	2 Cor. 5:16-21
Monday	Morning Psalm: 126		Evening Psalm: 8
	Eccles. 3:1-15	Mark 7:24-37	Col. 3:12-17
Tuesday	Morning Psalm: 73		Evening Psalm: 4
	Eccles 3:16-4:3	Mark 8:1-10	Heb. 9:11-15
Wednesday	Morning Psalm: 119:121-152		Evening Psalm: 119:163-176
	Eccles. 4:4-16	Mark 8:11-26	Heb. 10:19-25
Thursday	Morning Psalm: 76		Evening Psalm: 141
	Eccles. 5:1-7	Mark 8:27-9:1	Eph. 4:17-24
Friday	Morning Psalm: 58		Evening Psalm: 12
	Eccles. 5:8-20	Mark 9:2-13	Rom. 1:16-23
Saturday	Morning Psalm: 17		Evening Psalm: 7
	Eccles. 6:1-12	Mark 9:14-29	Rom. 3:21-26

Year C

Lent 5

Sunday	Morning Psalm: 120		Evening Psalm: 116
	Isa. 43:16-21	John 12:1-8	Phil. 3:8-14
Monday	Morning Psalm: 90		Evening Psalm: 7
	Eccles. 7:1-14	Mark 9:30-41	Phil. 3:15-4:1
Tuesday	Morning Psalm: 19		Evening Psalm: 91
	Eccles. 8:14-9:10	Mark 9:42-50	1 Cor. 9:19-27
Wednesday	Morning Psalm: 37		Evening Psalm: 112
	Eccles. 9:11-18	Mark 10:1-16	1 Cor. 15:20-28
Thursday	Morning Psalm: 62		Evening Psalm: 139
	Eccles. 11:1-8	Mark 10:17-31	2 Cor. 3:7-18
Friday	Morning Psalm: 54		Evening Psalm: 59
	Eccles. 11:9-12:14	Mark 10:32-45	2 Cor. 4:1-12
Saturday	Morning Psalm: 36		Evening Psalm: 48
	Zech. 9:9-12	Mark 10:46-52	2 Cor. 4:13-18

Holy Week
Passion/Palm Sunday

	Morning Psalm: 24		Evening Psalm: 31
	Isa. 50:4-9a	Luke 22:14-23:56 or Luke 19:28-40	Phil. 2:5-11
Monday	Morning Psalm: 87		Evening Psalm: 36
	Isa. 42:1-9	John 12:1-11	Heb. 9:11-15
Tuesday	Morning Psalm: 71		Evening Psalm: 27
	Isa. 49:1-7	John 12:20-36	1 Cor. 1:18-31
Wednesday	Morning Psalm: 70		Evening Psalm: 55
	Isa. 50:4-9a	John 13:21-30	Heb. 12:1-3

Maundy Thursday

Morning Psalm: 89:1-22   Evening Psalm: 89:23-48
Jer. 31:31-34   Luke 22:7-20   Heb. 10:16-25

Good Friday

Morning Psalm: 22:1-18   Evening Psalm: 22:19-31
Isa. 52:13-53:12   John 18:1-19:42 or John 19:17-30   Heb. 4:14-16; 5:7-9

Holy Saturday

Morning Psalm: 69:1-15   Evening Psalm: 69:16-36
Exod. 14:10-15:18   Luke 24:1-12   Rom. 6:3-11

A Daily Lectionary

Easter Sunday

Sunday	Morning Psalm: 150		Evening Psalm: 118
	Acts 10:34-43 or	John 20:1-18 or	1 Cor. 15:19-26 or
	Isa. 65:17-25	Luke 24:1-12	Acts 10:34-43
Monday	Morning Psalm: 77		Evening Psalm: 142
	Jon. 2:1-9	Mark 16:1-8	1 Cor. 15:1-11
Tuesday	Morning Psalm: 80		Evening Psalm: 74
	Isa. 30:18-21	Mark 16:9-20	1 Cor. 15:12-28
Wednesday	Morning Psalm: 149		Evening Psalm: 55
	Mic. 7:7-15	Matt. 28:1-10	1 Cor. 15:30-41
Thursday	Morning Psalm: 104:1-18		Evening Psalm: 104:19-35
	Ezek. 37:1-14	Matt. 28:11-20	1 Cor. 15:41-50
Friday	Morning Psalm: 98		Evening Psalm: 20
	Isa. 25:1-9	Luke 24:1-12	1 Cor. 15:51-58
Saturday	Morning Psalm: 21		Evening Psalm: 111
	Isa. 43:8-13	Mark 12:18-27	2 Cor. 4:16-5:10

Easter 2

Sunday	Morning Psalm: 148		Evening Psalm: 16
	Acts 5:27-32	John 20:19-31	Rev. 1:4-8
Monday	Morning Psalm: 92		Evening Psalm: 85
	Exod. 12:1-14	John 8:12-30	Rev. 1:1-3, 9-16
Tuesday	Morning Psalm: 78:1-31		Evening Psalm: 78:32-72
	Exod. 12:14-17	John 8:31-47	Rev. 1:17-20
Wednesday	Morning Psalm: 75		Evening Psalm: 136
	Exod. 12:28-39	John 8:48-59	Rev. 2:1-7
Thursday	Morning Psalm: 121		Evening Psalm: 13
	Exod. 12:40-51	John 9:1-17	Rev. 2:8-11
Friday	Morning Psalm: 105:1-22		Evening Psalm: 105:23-45
	Exod. 13:3-10	John 9:18-41	Rev. 2:12-17
Saturday	Morning Psalm: 140		Evening Psalm: 125
	Exod. 13:11-16	John 10:1-18	Rev. 2:18-29

Year C

Easter 3

Sunday	Morning Psalm: 116		Evening Psalm: 123
	Acts 9:1-20	John 21:1-19	Rev. 5:11-14
Monday	Morning Psalm: 135		Evening Psalm: 138
	Exod. 13:17-14:4	John 10:19-30	Rev. 3:1-6
Tuesday	Morning Psalm: 34		Evening Psalm: 83
	Exod. 14:5-22	John 10:31-42	Rev. 3:7-13
Wednesday	Morning Psalm: 96		Evening Psalm: 9
	Exod. 14:21-31	John 11:1-16	Rev. 3:14-22
Thursday	Morning Psalm: 102		Evening Psalm: 114
	Exod. 15:1-21	John 11:17-29	Rev. 4:1-11
Friday	Morning Psalm: 147		Evening Psalm: 106:1-23
	Exod. 15:22-16:10	John 11:30-44	Rev. 5:1-10
Saturday	Morning Psalm: 41		Evening Psalm: 106:24-48
	Exod. 16:10-22	John 11:45-54	Rev. 5:11-14

Easter 4

Sunday	Morning Psalm: 100		Evening Psalm: 23
	Acts 13:15-16, 26, 33	John 10:22-30	Rev. 7:9-17
Monday	Morning Psalm: 25		Evening Psalm: 46
	Exod. 16:23-36	John 11:55-12:8	Rev. 6:1-6
Tuesday	Morning Psalm: 118		Evening Psalm: 132
	Exod. 17:1-16	John 12:9-19	Rev. 6:7-11
Wednesday	Morning Psalm: 15		Evening Psalm: 53
	Exod. 18:1-12	John 12:20-26	Rev. 6:12-17
Thursday	Morning Psalm: 42		Evening Psalm: 82
	Exod. 18:13-27	John 12:27-36a	Rev. 7:1-8
Friday	Morning Psalm: 146		Evening Psalm: 33
	Exod. 19:1-16	John 12:36b-50	Rev. 7:9-17
Saturday	Morning Psalm: 55		Evening Psalm: 81
	Exod. 19:16-25	John 13:1-20	Rev. 8:1-6

A Daily Lectionary

Easter 5

Sunday	Morning Psalm: 131 Acts 14:8-18	John 13:31-35	Evening Psalm: 31 Rev. 21:1-6
Monday	Morning Psalm: 1 Exod. 20:1-21	John 13:21-30	Evening Psalm: 86 Rev. 8:7-13
Tuesday	Morning Psalm: 133 Exod. 24:1-18	John 13:31-38	Evening Psalm: 14 Rev. 9:1-11
Wednesday	Morning Psalm: 122 Exod. 25:1-22	John 14:1-7	Evening Psalm: 84 Rev. 9:12-21
Thursday	Morning Psalm: 101 Exod. 32:1-20	John 14:8-17	Evening Psalm: 94 Rev. 10:1-11
Friday	Morning Psalm: 24 Exod. 32:21-34	John 14:18-31	Evening Psalm: 143 Rev. 11:1-6
Saturday	Morning Psalm: 38 Exod. 34:1-17	John 15:1-11	Evening Psalm: 86 Rev. 11:7-14

Easter 6

Sunday	Morning Psalm: 66 Acts 15:1-2, 22-29	John 14:23-29	Evening Psalm: 113 Rev. 21:10, 22-27
Monday	Morning Psalm: 1 Exod. 34:18-35	John 15:12-27	Evening Psalm: 112 Rev. 12:1-6
Tuesday	Morning Psalm: 10 Exod. 40:18-38	John 16:1-15	Evening Psalm: 48 Rev. 12:7-12
Wednesday	Morning Psalm: 109 Dan. 7:9-14	John 16:16-33	Evening Psalm: 64 Eph. 1:1-10
Ascension Day	Morning Psalm: 47 Acts 1:1-11	Luke 24:46-53 or Mark 16:8-16, 19, 20	Evening Psalm: 110 Eph. 1:15-23
Friday	Morning Psalm: 137 Ezek. 1:1-14	John 17:1-11	Evening Psalm: 60 Rev. 12:13-17
Saturday	Morning Psalm: 27 Ezek. 1:15-28a	John 17:12-19	Evening Psalm: 44 Rev. 13:1-10

Year C

Easter 7
Sunday	Morning Psalm: 45		Evening Psalm: 68
	Acts 16:16-34	John 17:20-26	Rev. 22:12-14, 16-17, 20
Monday	Morning Psalm: 1		Evening Psalm: 19
	Deut. 13:1-5	John 3:31-36	Rev. 13:11-18
Tuesday	Morning Psalm: 119:1-24		Evening Psalm: 119:25-48
	Josh. 1:1-9	John 7:37-39	Rev. 14:1-11
Wednesday	Morning Psalm: 78:56-72		Evening Psalm: 132
	1 Sam. 16:1-13a	Luke 10:17-24	Rev. 14:12-20
Thursday	Morning Psalm: 72		Evening Psalm: 84
	Isa. 4:2-6	Luke 11:5-13	Acts 2:1-13
Friday	Morning Psalm: 118		Evening Psalm: 20
	Zech. 4:1-14	Luke 24:36-49	Acts 2:14-21
Saturday	Morning Psalm: 16		Evening Psalm: 129
	Deut. 16:9-12	John 20:19-23	Acts 2:22-28

Pentecost Sunday
Sunday	Morning Psalm: 104:1-18		Evening Psalm: 104:19-35
	Acts 2:1-21 or Gen. 11:1-9	John 14:8-17, 25-27	Rom. 8:14-17 or Acts 2:1-21
Monday	Morning Psalm: 40		Evening Psalm: 139
	Isa. 11:1-9	John 14:25-31	Acts 2:29-36
Tuesday	Morning Psalm: 65		Evening Psalm: 121
	Isa. 44:1-8	Matt. 13:1-17	Acts 2:37-42
Wednesday	Morning Psalm: 105:1-22		Evening Psalm: 105:23-45
	Deut. 4:1-14	Matt. 13:18-23	Acts 2:43-47
Thursday	Morning Psalm: 135		Evening Psalm: 115
	Deut. 4:15-31	Matt. 13:24-30	Rom. 7:1-6
Friday	Morning Psalm: 119:1-24		Evening Psalm: 119:25-48
	Deut.4:32-40	Matt. 13:31-35	Rom. 7:7-12
Saturday	Morning Psalm: 119:49-72		Evening Psalm: 119:73-96
	Deut. 6:1-15	John 1:29-34	Rom. 7:13-20

A Daily Lectionary

Trinity Sunday

Sunday	Morning Psalm: 90		Evening Psalm: 19
	Prov. 8:22-31	John 16:12-15	Rom. 5:1-5
Monday	Morning Psalm: 119:97-120		Evening Psalm: 119:121-152
	Job 28:12-28	Matt. 13:36-43	Rom. 7:21-25
Tuesday	Morning Psalm: 119:153-176		Evening Psalm: 1
	Job 38:1-11, 42:1-5	Matt. 13:44-52	Rom. 8:1-8
Wednesday	Morning Psalm: 89:1-23		Evening Psalm: 89:24-52
	1 Kings 1:(1-4) 5-31	Matt. 13:53-58	Rom. 8:9-17
Thursday	Morning Psalm: 132		Evening Psalm: 78:1-31
	1 Kings 1:32-2:4	Matt. 14:1-12	Rom. 8:18-25
Friday	Morning Psalm: 21		Evening Psalm: 78:32-72
	1 Kings 2:5-25	Matt. 14:13-21	Rom. 8:26-30
Saturday	Morning Psalm: 93		Evening Psalm: 29
	1 Kings 2:26-46	Matt. 14:22-36	Rom. 8:31-39

Proper 4 (*Sunday between May 29 and June 4 if after Trinity Sunday*)*

Sunday	Morning Psalm: 30		Evening Psalm: 117
	1 Kings 8:22-23, 41-43	Luke 7:1-10	Gal. 1:1-10
Monday	Morning Psalm: 72		Evening Psalm: 31
	1 Kings 3:1-15	Matt. 15:1-20	Gal. 1:11-17
Tuesday	Morning Psalm: 25		Evening Psalm: 34
	1 Kings 3:16-28	Matt. 15:21-28	Gal. 1:18-24
Wednesday	Morning Psalm: 87		Evening Psalm: 84
	1 Kings 5:1-6:7	Matt. 15:29-39	Gal. 2:1-10
Thursday	Morning Psalm: 122		Evening Psalm: 48
	1 Kings 7:51-8:21	Matt. 16:1-12	Gal. 2:11-21
Friday	Morning Psalm: 103		Evening Psalm: 81
	1 Kings 8:22-30 (31-40)	Matt. 16:13-20	Gal. 3:1-5
Saturday	Morning Psalm: 102		Evening Psalm: 136
	1 Kings 8:41-61	Matt. 16:21-28	Gal. 3:6-14

**If the Sunday between May 24 and 28 follows Trinity Sunday, go back to Proper 3.*

Year C

Proper 5 (*Sunday between June 5 and 11 if after Trinity Sunday*)

Sunday	Morning Psalm: 150		Evening Psalm: 134
	1 Kings 17:17-24	Luke 7:11-17	Gal. 1:11-24
Monday	Morning Psalm: 2		Evening Psalm: 97
	1 Kings 8:62-9:9	Matt. 17:1-13	Gal. 3:15-20
Tuesday	Morning Psalm: 72		Evening Psalm: 68
	1 Kings 9:24-10:13	Matt. 17:14-21	Gal. 3:21-29
Wednesday	Morning Psalm: 38		Evening Psalm: 32
	1 Kings 11:1-13	Matt. 17:22-27	Gal. 4:1-7
Thursday	Morning Psalm: 79		Evening Psalm: 106:1-23
	1 Kings 11:26-43	Matt. 18:1-9	Gal. 4:8-14
Friday	Morning Psalm: 106:24-48		Evening Psalm: 74
	1 Kings 12:1-20	Matt. 18:10-20	Gal. 4:15-20
Saturday	Morning Psalm: 135		Evening Psalm: 115
	1 Kings 12:21-33	Matt. 18:21-35	Gal. 4:21-31

Proper 6 (*Sunday between June 12 and 18 if after Trinity Sunday*)

Sunday	Morning Psalm: 149		Evening Psalm: 8
	1 Kings 19:1-8	Luke 7:36-8:3	Gal. 2:15-21
Monday	Morning Psalm: 45		Evening Psalm: 128
	1 Kings 13:1-10	Matt. 19:1-12	Acts 9:32-43
Tuesday	Morning Psalm: 17		Evening Psalm: 49
	1 Kings 13:11-32	Matt. 19:13-22	Acts 10:1-8
Wednesday	Morning Psalm: 50		Evening Psalm: 62
	1 Kings 13:33-14:20	Matt. 19:23-30	Acts 10:9-16
Thursday	Morning Psalm: 145		Evening Psalm: 86
	1 Kings 16:23-34	Matt. 20:1-16	Acts 10:17-23
Friday	Morning Psalm: 146		Evening Psalm: 66
	1 Kings 17:1-24	Matt. 20:17-28	Acts 10:24-33
Saturday	Morning Psalm: 3		Evening Psalm: 27
	1 Kings 18:1-19	Matt. 20:29-34	Acts 10:34-43

A Daily Lectionary

Proper 7 (*Sunday between June 19 and 25 if after Trinity Sunday*)

Sunday	Morning Psalm: 148		Evening Psalm: 128
	1 Kings 19:9-14	Luke 9:18-24	Gal. 3:23-29
Monday	Morning Psalm: 24		Evening Psalm: 118
	1 Kings 18:20-40	Matt. 21:1-11	Acts 10:44-48
Tuesday	Morning Psalm: 11		Evening Psalm: 8
	1 Kings 18:41-19:8	Matt. 21:12-22	Acts 11:1-9
Wednesday	Morning Psalm: 51		Evening Psalm: 4
	1 Kings 19:8-21	Matt. 21:23-32	Acts 11:10-13
Thursday	Morning Psalm: 80		Evening Psalm: 14
	1 Kings 21:1-16	Matt. 21:33-46	Acts 11:19-26
Friday	Morning Psalm: 88		Evening Psalm: 53
	1 Kings 21:17-29	Matt. 22:1-14	Acts 11:27-12:5
Saturday	Morning Psalm: 54		Evening Psalm: 39
	1 Kings 22:1-28	Matt. 22:15-22	Acts 12:6-17

Proper 8 (*Sunday between June 26 and July 2 inclusive*)

Sunday	Morning Psalm: 109		Evening Psalm: 58
	1 Kings 19:15-21	Luke 9:51-62	Gal. 5:1, 13-25
Monday	Morning Psalm: 83		Evening Psalm: 16
	1 Kings 22:29-45 (46-53)	Matt. 22:23-40	Acts 12:18-25
Tuesday	Morning Psalm: 52		Evening Psalm: 46
	2 Kings 1:2-17	Matt. 23:1-12	Gal. 5:1-6
Wednesday	Morning Psalm: 61		Evening Psalm: 33
	2 Kings 2:1-25	Matt. 23:13-26	Gal. 5:7-12
Thursday	Morning Psalm: 92		Evening Psalm: 40
	2 Kings 3:1-20	Matt. 23:27-39	Gal. 5:13-18
Friday	Morning Psalm: 96		Evening Psalm: 94
	2 Kings 3:21-4:7	Matt. 24:1-14	Gal. 5:19-26
Saturday	Morning Psalm: 98		Evening Psalm: 60
	2 Kings 4:8-37	Matt. 24:15-31	Gal. 6:1-6

Year C

Proper 9 (*Sunday between July 3 and 9 inclusive*)

Sunday	Morning Psalm: 147 1 Kings 21:1-3, 17-21	Luke 10:1-12, 17-20	Evening Psalm: 73 Gal. 6:7-18
Monday	Morning Psalm: 41 2 Kings 4:38-5:14	Matt. 24:32-51	Evening Psalm: 112 Col. 1:1-8
Tuesday	Morning Psalm: 82 2 Kings 5:15-27	Matt. 25:1-13	Evening Psalm: 141 Col. 1:9-14
Wednesday	Morning Psalm: 99 2 Kings 6:1-23	Matt. 25:14-30	Evening Psalm: 91 Col. 1:15-20
Thursday	Morning Psalm: 101 2 Kings 6:24-7:2	Matt. 25:31-46	Evening Psalm: 75 Col. 1:21-29
Friday	Morning Psalm: 56 2 Kings 7:3-20	Matt. 26:1-16	Evening Psalm: 55 Col. 2:1-7
Saturday	Morning Psalm: 57 2 Kings 8:1-19	Matt. 26:17-25	Evening Psalm: 4 Col. 2:8-15

Proper 10 (*Sunday between July 10 and 16 inclusive*)

Sunday	Morning Psalm: 76 2 Kings 2:1, 6-14	Luke 10:25-37	Evening Psalm: 77 Col. 1:1-14
Monday	Morning Psalm: 71 2 Kings 9:1-16	Matt. 26:26-35	Evening Psalm: 59 Acts 3:1-10
Tuesday	Morning Psalm: 6 2 Kings 9:17-37	Matt. 26:36-46	Evening Psalm: 64 Acts 3:11-16
Wednesday	Morning Psalm: 70 2 Kings 10:1-15	Matt. 26:47-56	Evening Psalm: 10 Acts 3:17-24
Thursday	Morning Psalm: 110 2 Kings 10:16-36	Matt. 26:57-68	Evening Psalm: 35 Acts 3:25-4:4
Friday	Morning Psalm: 12 2 Kings 11:1-21	Matt. 26:69-75	Evening Psalm: 13 Acts 4:5-12
Saturday	Morning Psalm: 17 2 Kings 12:1-16	Matt. 27:1-10	Evening Psalm: 26 Acts 4:13-22

A Daily Lectionary

Proper 11 (*Sunday between July 17 and 23 inclusive*)

Sunday	Morning Psalm: 63		Evening Psalm: 34
	2 Kings 4:8-17	Luke 10:38-42	Col. 1:21-29
Monday	Morning Psalm: 120		Evening Psalm: 28
	2 Kings 13:14-23	Matt. 27:11-23	Acts 4:23-31
Tuesday	Morning Psalm: 69:1-15		Evening Psalm: 69:16-36
	2 Kings 17:1-20	Matt. 27:24-31	Acts 4:32-37
Wednesday	Morning Psalm: 22:1-15		Evening Psalm: 22:16-31
	2 Kings 17:21-41	Matt. 27:32-44	Col. 2:16-23
Thursday	Morning Psalm: 42		Evening Psalm: 43
	2 Kings 18:9-25	Matt. 27:45-54	Col. 3:1-11
Friday	Morning Psalm: 20		Evening Psalm: 85
	2 Kings 18:26-37	Mat. 27:55-66	Col. 3:12-17
Saturday	Morning Psalm: 21		Evening Psalm: 47
	2 Kings 19:1-20	Matt. 28:1-10	Col. 3:18-24

Proper 12 (*Sunday between July 24 and 30 inclusive*)

Sunday	Morning Psalm: 107:1-22		Evening Psalm: 107:23-43
	2 Kings 5:1-15b	Luke 11:1-13	Col. 2:6-15
Monday	Morning Psalm: 67		Evening Psalm: 111
	2 Kings 19:21-36	Matt. 28:11-20	Col. 4:1-9
Tuesday	Morning Psalm: 108		Evening Psalm: 125
	2 Kings 20:1-21	Luke 1:1-25	Col. 4:10-18
Wednesday	Morning Psalm: 36		Evening Psalm: 123
	2 Kings 21:1-18	Luke 1:26-38	Acts 5:1-11
Thursday	Morning Psalm: 116		Evening Psalm: 127
	2 Kings 22:1-13	Luke 1:39-48a	Acts 5:12-21a
Friday	Morning Psalm: 138		Evening Psalm: 113
	2 Kings 22:14-23:3	Luke 1:48-56	Acts 5:21b-32
Saturday	Morning Psalm: 124		Evening Psalm: 136
	2 Kings 23:4-27	Luke 1:57-66	Acts 5:33-42

Year C

Proper 13 (*Sunday between July 31 and August 6 inclusive*)

Sunday	Morning Psalm: 5		Evening Psalm: 7
	2 Kings 13:14-20a	Luke 12:13-21	Col. 3:1-11
Monday	Morning Psalm: 18:1-24		Evening Psalm: 18:25-50
	2 Kings 23:36-24:17	Luke 1:67-80	Acts 6:1-7
Tuesday	Morning Psalm: 131		Evening Psalm: 95
	2 Kings 25:1-17	Luke 2:1-14	Acts 6:8-15
Wednesday	Morning Psalm: 126		Evening Psalm: 114
	2 Kings 25:18-30	Luke 2:15-21	Acts 7:1-8
Thursday	Morning Psalm: 144		Evening Psalm: 139
	Jer. 1:1-10	Luke 2:22-32	Acts 7:9-16
Friday	Morning Psalm: 143		Evening Psalm: 142
	Jer. 1:11-19	Luke 2:33-40	Acts 7:17-29
Saturday	Morning Psalm: 15		Evening Psalm: 48
	Jer. 2:1-13	Luke 2:41-52	Acts 7:30-40

Proper 14 (*Sunday between August 7 and 13 inclusive*)

Sunday	Morning Psalm: 137		Evening Psalm: 79
	Jer. 18:1-11	Luke 12:32-40	Heb. 11:1-3, 8-19
Monday	Morning Psalm: 87		Evening Psalm: 84
	Jer. 3:6-18	Luke 3:1-14	Acts 7:41-50
Tuesday	Morning Psalm: 15		Evening Psalm: 129
	Jer. 4:9-28	Luke 3:15-22	Acts 7:51-8:1a
Wednesday	Morning Psalm: 130		Evening Psalm: 95
	Jer. 5:1-9	Luke 3:21-38	Heb. 11:4-7, 20-22
Thursday	Morning Psalm: 14		Evening Psalm: 53
	Jer. 5:20-31	Luke 4:1-13	Heb. 11:23-31
Friday	Morning Psalm: 140		Evening Psalm: 33
	Jer. 6:9-15	Luke 4:14-21	Heb. 11:32-40
Saturday	Morning Psalm: 24		Evening Psalm: 15
	Jer. 7:1-15	Luke 4:22-30	Heb. 12:3-11

A Daily Lectionary

Proper 15 (*Sunday between August 14 and 20 inclusive*)

Sunday	Morning Psalm: 100		Evening Psalm: 23
	Jer. 20:7-13	Luke 12:49-56	Heb. 12:1-2, 12, 17
Monday	Morning Psalm: 78:1-31		Evening Psalm: 78:32-72
	Jer. 7:21-34	Luke 4:31-37	Heb. 12:12-17
Tuesday	Morning Psalm: 106:1-23		Evening Psalm: 106:24-48
	Jer. 8:18-9:6	Luke 4:38-44	Heb. 12:18-24
Wednesday	Morning Psalm: 29		Evening Psalm: 135
	Jer. 10:11-24	Luke 5:1-11	Heb. 12:25-29
Thursday	Morning Psalm: 19		Evening Psalm: 81
	Jer. 11:1-20	Luke 5:12-26	Heb. 13:1-6
Friday	Morning Psalm: 45		Evening Psalm: 68
	Jer. 13:1-11	Luke 5:27-39	Heb. 13:7-14
Saturday	Morning Psalm: 32		Evening Psalm: 14
	Jer. 14:7-22	Luke 6:1-11	Heb. 13:15-25

Proper 16 (*Sunday between August 21 and 27 inclusive*)

Sunday	Morning Psalm: 10		Evening Psalm: 31
	Jer. 28:1-9	Luke 13:22-30	Heb. 12:18-29
Monday	Morning Psalm: 106:1-23		Evening Psalm: 106:24-48
	Jer. 16:10-21	Luke 6:12-26	Acts 8:1b-8
Tuesday	Morning Psalm: 54		Evening Psalm: 35
	Jer. 17:14-27	Luke 6:27-38	Acts 8:9-13
Wednesday	Morning Psalm: 72		Evening Psalm: 37
	Jer. 22:13-23	Luke 6:39-49	Acts 8:14-24
Thursday	Morning Psalm: 100		Evening Psalm: 23
	Jer. 23:1-8	Luke 7:1-17	Acts 8:25-31
Friday	Morning Psalm: 58		Evening Psalm: 14
	Jer. 23:9-15	Luke 7:18-35	Acts 8:32-40
Saturday	Morning Psalm: 29		Evening Psalm: 139
	Jer. 23:16-32	Luke 7:36-50	Acts 9:1-9

Year C

Proper 17 (*Sunday between August 28 and September 3 inclusive*)

Sunday	Morning Psalm: 150		Evening Psalm: 84
	Ezek. 18:1-9, 25-29	Luke 14:1, 7-14	Heb. 13:1-8
Monday	Morning Psalm: 119:1-24		Evening Psalm: 119:25-48
	Ezek. 1:1-14	Luke 8:1-15	Acts 9:10-19a
Tuesday	Morning Psalm: 93		Evening Psalm: 114
	Ezek. 1:15-28	Luke 8:16-25	Acts 9:19b-31
Wednesday	Morning Psalm: 61		Evening Psalm: 43
	Ezek. 2:1-3:3	Luke 8:26-39	Rev. 15:1-8
Thursday	Morning Psalm: 102		Evening Psalm: 7
	Ezek. 3:4-17	Luke 8:40-56	Rev. 16:1-11
Friday	Morning Psalm: 116		Evening Psalm: 64
	Ezek. 3:16-27	Luke 9:1-17	Rev. 16:12-21
Saturday	Morning Psalm: 119:49-72		Evening Psalm: 119:73-96
	Ezek. 4:1-17	Luke 9:18-27	Rev. 17:1-6a

Proper 18 (*Sunday between September 4 and 10 inclusive*)

Sunday	Morning Psalm: 15		Evening Psalm: 79
	Ezek. 33:1-11	Luke 14:25-33	Philem. 1-20
Monday	Morning Psalm: 119:97-120		Evening Psalm: 74
	Ezek. 7:10-27	Luke 9:28-36	Rev. 17:6b-18
Tuesday	Morning Psalm: 137		Evening Psalm: 80
	Ezek. 11:14-25	Luke 9:37-50	Rev. 18:1-8
Wednesday	Morning Psalm: 53		Evening Psalm: 81
	Ezek. 16:1-22	Luke 9:51-62	Rev. 18:9-14
Thursday	Morning Psalm: 52		Evening Psalm: 27
	Ezek. 16:35-52	Luke 10:1-16	Rev. 18:15-24
Friday	Morning Psalm: 136		Evening Psalm: 129
	Ezek. 16:53-63	Luke 10:17-24	Rev. 19:1-10
Saturday	Morning Psalm: 38		Evening Psalm: 32
	Ezek. 23:1-21	Luke 10:25-37	Rev. 19:11-21

A Daily Lectionary

Proper 19 (*Sunday between September 11 and 17 inclusive*)

Sunday	Morning Psalm: 25		Evening Psalm: 94
	Hos. 4:1-3, 5:15-6:6	Luke 15:1-10	1 Tim. 1:12-17
Monday	Morning Psalm: 51		Evening Psalm: 117
	Ezek. 23:36-49	Luke 10:38-42	Rev. 20:1-6
Tuesday	Morning Psalm: 78:1-31		Evening Psalm: 78:32-72
	Ezek. 34:17-31	Luke 11:1-13	Rev. 20:7-15
Wednesday	Morning Psalm: 122		Evening Psalm: 112
	Ezek. 43:1-12	Luke 11:14-26	Rev. 21:1-8
Thursday	Morning Psalm: 87		Evening Psalm: 1
	Hos. 1:1-2:1	Luke 11:27-36	Rev. 21:9-17
Friday	Morning Psalm: 50		Evening Psalm: 40
	Hos. 2:2-14	Luke 11:37-52	Rev. 21:18-27
Saturday	Morning Psalm: 16		Evening Psalm: 11
	Hos. 2:14-23	Luke 11:53-12:12	Rev. 22:1-7

Proper 20 (*Sunday between September 18 and 24 inclusive*)

Sunday	Morning Psalm: 119:153-176		Evening Psalm: 77
	Hos. 11:1-11	Luke 16:1-13	1 Tim. 2:1-7
Monday	Morning Psalm: 49		Evening Psalm: 39
	Hos. 4:1-10	Luke 12:13-31	Rev. 22:8-15
Tuesday	Morning Psalm: 36		Evening Psalm: 73
	Hos. 4:11-19	Luke 12:32-48	Rev. 22:16-21
Wednesday	Morning Psalm: 30		Evening Psalm: 19
	Hos. 5:8-6:6	Luke 12:49-59	Rom. 1:1-15
Thursday	Morning Psalm: 80		Evening Psalm: 12
	Hos. 10:1-15	Luke 13:1-9	Rom. 1:16-25
Friday	Morning Psalm: 67		Evening Psalm: 85
	Hos. 11:1-9	Luke 13:10-17	Rom. 1:26-32
Saturday	Morning Psalm: 17		Evening Psalm: 91
	Hos. 14:1-9	Luke 13:18-30	Rom. 2:1-11

Year C

Proper 21 (*Sunday between September 25 and October 1 inclusive*)

Sunday	Morning Psalm: 107:1-22		Evening Psalm: 107:23-43
	Joel 2:23-30	Luke 16:19-31	1 Tim. 6:6-19
Monday	Morning Psalm: 63		Evening Psalm: 42
	Joel 1:1-14	Luke 13:31-35	Rom. 2:12-16
Tuesday	Morning Psalm: 75		Evening Psalm: 82
	Joel 1:15-2:11	Luke 14:1-11	Rom. 2:17-24
Wednesday	Morning Psalm: 147		Evening Psalm: 44
	Joel 2:12-19	Luke 14:12-24	Rom. 2:25-26
Thursday	Morning Psalm: 149		Evening Psalm: 34
	Joel 2:21-27	Luke 14:25-35	Rom. 2:27-3:18
Friday	Morning Psalm: 18:1-24		Evening Psalm: 18:25-50
	Joel 2:28-3:8	Luke 15:1-10	Rom. 3:19-31
Saturday	Morning Psalm: 47		Evening Psalm: 46
	Joel 3:9-17	Luke 15:11-32	Rom. 4:1-12

Proper 22 (*Sunday between October 2 and 8 inclusive*)

Sunday	Morning Psalm: 148		Evening Psalm: 8
	Amos 6:5-7, 10-15	Luke 17:5-10	2 Tim. 1:1-14
Monday	Morning Psalm: 5		Evening Psalm: 24
	Mic. 1:1-9	Luke 16:1-9	Rom. 4:13-18
Tuesday	Morning Psalm: 120		Evening Psalm: 28
	Mic. 2:1-13	Luke 16:10-18	Rom. 4:19-25
Wednesday	Morning Psalm: 18:1-24		Evening Psalm: 18:25-50
	Mic. 3:1-8	Luke 16:19-31	Rom. 5:1-5
Thursday	Morning Psalm: 122		Evening Psalm: 48
	Mic. 3:9-4:5	Luke 17:1-10	Rom. 5:6-11
Friday	Morning Psalm: 62		Evening Psalm: 138
	Mic. 5:1-4, 10-15	Luke 17:11-19	Rom. 5:12-21
Saturday	Morning Psalm: 15		Evening Psalm: 24
	Mic. 6:1-8	Luke 17:20-37	Rom. 6:1-11

A Daily Lectionary

Proper 23 (*Sunday between October 9 and 15 inclusive*)

Sunday	Morning Psalm: 101 Mic. 1:2, 2:1-10	Luke 17:11-19	Evening Psalm: 14 2 Tim. 2:8-15
Monday	Morning Psalm: 146 Mic. 7:1-7	Luke 18:1-8	Evening Psalm: 53 Rom. 6:12-19
Tuesday	Morning Psalm: 92 Mic. 7:8-20	Luke 18:9-14	Evening Psalm: 99 Rom. 6:20-23
Wednesday	Morning Psalm: 90 Hab. 1:1-17	Luke 18:13-30	Evening Psalm: 13 Rom. 7:1-6
Thursday	Morning Psalm: 27 Hab. 2:1-11	Luke 18:31-43	Evening Psalm: 141 Rom. 7:7-12
Friday	Morning Psalm: 135 Hab. 2:12-20	Luke 19:1-10	Evening Psalm: 115 Rom. 7:13-20
Saturday	Morning Psalm: 98 Hab. 3:1-10 (11-19)	Luke 19:11-27	Evening Psalm: 68 Rom. 7:21-25

Proper 24 (*Sunday between October 16 and 22 inclusive*)

Sunday	Morning Psalm: 26 Hab. 1:1-3, 2:1-4	Luke 18:1-8	Evening Psalm: 6 2 Tim. 3:14-4:5
Monday	Morning Psalm: 76 Prov. 6:1-19	Luke 19:28-40	Evening Psalm: 118 Rom. 8:1-8
Tuesday	Morning Psalm: 87 Prov. 7:1-27	Luke 19:41-48	Evening Psalm: 48 Rom. 8:9-17
Wednesday	Morning Psalm: 57 Prov. 9:1-12	Luke 20:1-8	Evening Psalm: 56 Rom. 8:18-25
Thursday	Morning Psalm: 70 Prov. 10:1-12	Luke 20:9-18	Evening Psalm: 59 Rom. 8:26-30
Friday	Morning Psalm: 83 Zeph. 1:1-9	Luke 20:19-26	Evening Psalm: 4 Rom. 8:31-39
Saturday	Morning Psalm: 88 Zeph. 1:10-18	Luke 20:27-40	Evening Psalm: 86 Rom. 9:1-5

Year C

Proper 25 (*Sunday between October 23 and 29 inclusive*)

Sunday	Morning Psalm: 119:121-152		Evening Psalm: 134
	Zeph. 3:1-9	Luke 18:9-14	2 Tim. 4:6-8, 16-18
Monday	Morning Psalm: 50		Evening Psalm: 110
	Prov. 15:16-33	Luke 20:41-21:4	Rom. 9:6-13
Tuesday	Morning Psalm: 96		Evening Psalm: 97
	Prov. 17:1-20	Luke 21:5-19	Rom. 9:14-18
Wednesday	Morning Psalm: 108		Evening Psalm: 111
	Prov. 21:30-22:6	Luke 21:20-28	Rom. 9:19-27
Thursday	Morning Psalm: 123		Evening Psalm: 60
	Prov. 23:19-21, 29-24:2	Luke 21:29-38	Rom. 9:28-33
Friday	Morning Psalm: 41		Evening Psalm: 55
	Prov. 25:15-28	Luke 22:1-13	Rom. 10:1-4
Saturday	Morning Psalm: 89:1-24		Evening Psalm: 89:25-52
	Hag. 1:1-15	Luke 22:14-30	Rom. 10:5-9

Proper 26 (*Sunday between October 30 and November 5 inclusive*)

Sunday	Morning Psalm: 3		Evening Psalm: 122
	Hag. 2:1-9	Luke 19:1-10	2 Thess. 1:5-12
Monday	Morning Psalm: 144		Evening Psalm: 143
	Hag. 2:10-23	Luke 22:31-38	Rom. 10:10-16
Tuesday	Morning Psalm: 2		Evening Psalm: 33
	Zech. 1:17-27	Luke 22:39-53	Rom. 10:17-20
Wednesday	Morning Psalm: 71		Evening Psalm: 142
	Zech. 2:1-13	Luke 22:54-71	Rom. 10:21-11:6
Thursday	Morning Psalm: 69:1-15		Evening Psalm: 69:16-36
	Zech. 3:1-10	Luke 23:1-12	Rom. 11:7-12
Friday	Morning Psalm: 130		Evening Psalm: 31
	Zech. 4:1-14	Luke 23:13-25	Rom. 11:13-21
Saturday	Morning Psalm: 22:1-15		Evening Psalm: 22:16-31
	Zech. 5:1-11	Luke 23:26-31	Rom. 11:22-28

A Daily Lectionary

Proper 27 (*Sunday between November 6 and 12 inclusive*)

Sunday	Morning Psalm: 45 Zech. 7:1-10	Luke 20:27-38	Evening Psalm: 65 2 Thess. 2:13-3:5
Monday	Morning Psalm: 145 Zech. 6:1-15	Luke 23:32-43	Evening Psalm: 43 Rom. 11:29-36
Tuesday	Morning Psalm: 140 Zech. 7:8-8:8	Luke 23:44-56a	Evening Psalm: 35 Rom. 12:1-2
Wednesday	Morning Psalm: 21 Zech. 8:9-17	Luke 23:56b-24:11	Evening Psalm: 66 Rom. 12:3-8
Thursday	Morning Psalm: 132 Mal. 1:1-14	Luke 24:12-35	Evening Psalm: 121 Rom. 12:9-13
Friday	Morning Psalm: 118 Mal. 2:1-16	Luke 24:36-53	Evening Psalm: 126 Rom. 12:14-21
Saturday	Morning Psalm: 131 Mal. 3:1-12 (13-18)	Matt. 18:1-9	Evening Psalm: 133 2 John 1-13

Proper 28 (*Sunday between November 13 and 19 inclusive*)

Sunday	Morning Psalm: 9 Mal. 4:1-6	Luke 21:5-19	Evening Psalm: 117 2 Thess. 3:6-13
Monday	Morning Psalm: 100 Zech. 9:9-16	Matt. 18:10-20	Evening Psalm: 23 3 John 1-8
Tuesday	Morning Psalm: 103 Zech. 10:1-12	Matt. 18:21-35	Evening Psalm: 104 3 John 9-15
Wednesday	Morning Psalm: 20 Zech. 11:4-17	John 11:1-16	Evening Psalm: 124 Jude 1-13
Thursday	Morning Psalm: 109 Zech. 12:1-10	John 11:17-27	Evening Psalm: 125 Jude 14-25
Friday	Morning Psalm: 51 Zech. 13:1-9	John 11:28-44	Evening Psalm: 105 1 Cor. 3:10-23
Saturday	Morning Psalm: 97 Zech. 14:1-11	Matt. 20:1-16	Evening Psalm: 93 Phil. 2:1-11

Year C

Christ the King Sunday

Sunday	Morning Psalm: 47		Evening Psalm: 95
	2 Sam. 5:1-5	John 12:9-19	Col. 1:11-20
Monday	Morning Psalm: 105:1-22		Evening Psalm: 105:23-45
	Zech. 14:12-21	Matt. 20:17-28	Eph. 1:3-14
Tuesday	Morning Psalm: 27		Evening Psalm: 127
	Obad. 15-21	Matt. 20:29-34	Eph. 1:15-23
Wednesday	Morning Psalm: 18:1-24		Evening Psalm: 18:25-50
	Nah. 1:1-13	Matt. 24:1-14	Rev. 1:4-11
Thursday	Morning Psalm: 38		Evening Psalm: 128
	Isa. 1:1-9	Matt. 24:15-28	Rev. 1:12-20
Friday	Morning Psalm: 50		Evening Psalm: 15
	Isa. 1:10-20	Matt. 24:29-35	Rom. 13:1-7
Saturday	Morning Psalm: 87		Evening Psalm: 14
	Isa. 1:21-31	Matt. 24:46-51	Rom. 13:8-14

W. Douglas Mills is a United Methodist pastor in Taos, New Mexico. He has previously been a pastor in North Carolina, where he attended Duke University Divinity School and spent time as an intern at York Chapel.

Mr. Mills served as Registrar for the Consultation on Liturgy and Worship for the World Methodist Council, which met in Nairobi, Kenya, in July 1986. He is also an associate member of the Society of St. John the Evangelist.